Winging-it

by

Linda Varsell Smith

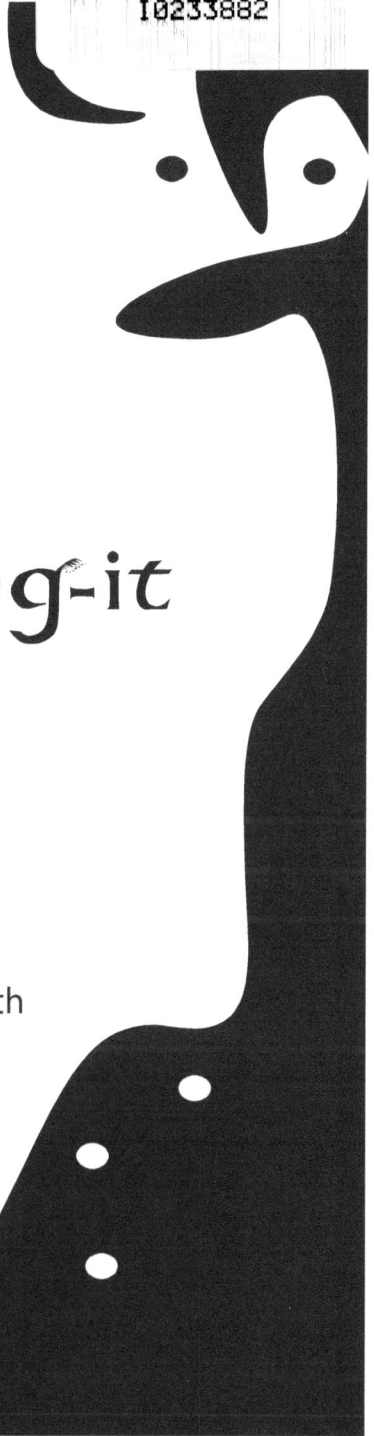

Thanks to:

Maureen Frank, the Mandala Lady for the cover art/design and
preparing the manuscript for printing.
www.TheMandalaLady.com

Joanna Rosinska of Primary Remiges for the frontispiece and
sectional artwork.

My poetry friends and family for their support

Rainbow Communications
471 NW Hemlock Ave.
Corvallis, Oregon 97330

www.rainbowcommunications.org

Contents

1- Introduction- Winging-It

Be like a bird that, pausing in her flight
awhile on bough to light,
feels them give way beneath her– and sings
knowing she hath wings.   Victor Hugo

-2 - Red Cape Capers

Even when muddy your wings sparkle bright wonders
that heal broken worlds. Aberjhani

-3- Cinqueries: A Cluster of Cinquos and Lanternes

Feet, what do I need you for when I have wings to fly? Frida Kahlo

-4- Fibs and Other Truths

I'm no angel, but I spread my wings a bit. Mae West.

-5- Black Stars on a White Sky

To stay ahead, you must have your next idea waiting in the wings.
Rosabeth Moss Kaner

-6- Poems That Count

A beautiful line of verse has twelve feet, and two wings.
Jules Renaro

-7- Poems That Count Too

Since words are all we have of wings.   Mark O'Connor

-8- Syllables of Velvet

Books allow you to take flight, unlike the chicken wings I stapled to my back before eating them. Jared Kintz

-9- Word-Playful

Jump, and you will find out how to unfold your wings as you fall.
Ray Bradbury

-10- Free Flying- Selected New Poems

Science begs literature to develop wings. Santosh Kalwar

-11- Angels

*The wings of angels are often found
on the backs of the least likely people. Eric Honeycutt*

*We are each of us angels with one wing;
and we can only fly by embracing one another. Luciano de Crescenzo*

Outside the open window the morning is awash with angels. Richard Wilbur

*Everyone entrusted with a mission is an angel. All forces that reside inside
the body are angels. Moses Maimonides*

*Yet I am the necessary angel of earth
since, in my sight, you see earth again. Wallace Stevens.*

-12- Departures

*You were born with wings.
Why prefer to crawl through life? Jalahad-din Rumi*

Winging-It

Winging-It   Introduction

I decided to wing it. That's the kind of player I am, just come out and wing it, so it worked again. Dwayne Wade

Winging A Poem

Reach
for words
winging to mind.

Place
pen on
paper, finger keys.

Play
with words
by hand moves.

Images
on screen
or paper line-up.

Erase
delete, shift
around and edit.

Poems
squiggle, writhe–
illusive before berth.

Hear
rhythm, form.
Words fill-in space.

Loosen
grip, reflect, pause,
then you'll dance.

Listen
to music–
compose your songlines.

Mused
words takeoff–
wing for flight.

Poetry Carnival

Thoughts spin
            like a merry-go-round
undulate like roller-coaster

circle like Ferris Wheel
            making me
                        dizzy.

Experimenting with Poetry Forms

Poetry seeks unique new forms
counting syllables, words, rhymes
foregoing meter for new norms
multi-cultural, modern times.

Natural speech patterns
are designing the page,
attention poet earns
not just current adage.

Freed poems fly
into your mind,
catch reader's eye.
eager to find.

Poet
re-shapes, re-forms.
Show it.
Poetry seeks unique new forms.

Syllabic Searches

Poetry is a search for syllables
to shoot at barriers of the unknown
Carl Sandburg says and the unknowable.
Figuring count is what makes poets groan,
miscounting worse, evokes dramatic moan.

Forms enable
pattern to flow, search for terse word.
Poetry is a search for syllables
in the best place, best sense, best heard,
inscrutable.

Syllables in metrics causes stresses,
language can contort, uncomfortable
metric feet can stumble into messes.
Both ways, steps down the line are stoppable.
Poetry is a search for syllables.

When You Write

Write a poem of light
so vision shines bright,
block dark words imprint,
let light words sprint,
win a mind raced
darkness chased
toward light.
Be free
to fly
wing
words
for flight,
land
thoughts
to
touch grounded experience.

Writingly

Write
wing-words.
swing, fling words,
bring words, cling words,
lingering, fingering words,
Mingling, tingling, jingling,
queen and king words, ping, zing words.
Hingeing, singeing, simmering, stinging words,
ring-a-ding, ding-a-ling, merry-wing words.

Quotes with Wings

When books are opened you discover that you have wings. Helen Hayes

May you always walk in sunshine. May you never want for more. May angels rest their wings right beside your door. Irish Blessing.

You can put wings on a pig, but you don't make it an eagle. Bill Clinton

The one without dreams is the one without wings. Muhammed Ali

But dear one, there are so many of us who don't have wings! You don't have any yourself, I notice. Would you like to try some?   Eve Neuhaus

I stood on the balcony with mourning hoping the earth would spread its wings in my uninhabited love. Pablo Neruda

Not so fast, not so high, without my wings, I cannot fly. Kelly Stracke

Our hours in love have wings; in absence, crutches. Miquel de Cervantes Saevedra

You cannot fly like an eagle with wings of a wren. William James.

Imprinting

Words are the fingerprints of the soul...Daniel Day-Lewis

Unfold the fist of spirit.
Unknuckle the hands from prayer.
Finger-mark words on the page—
inklings of the cloud of unknowing.

Imprint ideas from your meandering mind
to record your soul's journey.
Words are one way to finger the essence
of what remains intangible.

Red Cape Capers

Meditations

Contemplating in the Backyard

Greeting the sun splaying over the horizon,
leaves on the fruit trees under-lit with light,
I contemplate the dawning of a new day.
Wrapped in a red cape, sitting on a small angel pillow
balanced on my cane/stool, the chi of Gaia
enters my feet to energize my day.

The lawn is parched brown by summer
with green patches of residual spring.
Wormy apples plop to the ground
to be savored and wrapped by my husband,
to last beyond this autumnal season.
Each apple lovingly cut and cored
by him no matter how bruised or penetrated.

Migrating geese and other birds caw in the distance,
some unseen in the canopies of the hazelnut,
cherry, plum and apple trees.
The neighbors' dog barks, fainter barks respond.
No deer, raccoons or nutria detected.
The murmur and whir of nearby traffic
slurs sound and stirs my silence.
Lichen lick the crushed, cracked concrete wall.

As the light shifts, so do my thoughts.
I am new to this morning aubade
designed by a friend to renew my healing.
I am to visualize positive changes,
to connect to what I am to become.

Beads arc like rainbows over my watchband.
Time is up for this day.
I fold up the stool, carry pillow and cane into the house.
I hope my cape empowers me like Wonder Woman.

Attempting to Meditate

With my Buddha belly
and wearing a red cape
you would think I could reach
a magical, meditative state
in this autumnal garden.

But I am just a fat, old woman
shrouded in her mother's scarlet cape
distracted by the sights and sounds
of this browning backyard.

I sit on a metallic and plastic cane/stool
instead of sitting on the craggy, stone wall
wearing black, velcro-ed SAS shoes
not barefoot
creating boundaries
to absorbing Gaia's chi.

I am in a pink sweat suit
running from life, surfacing
instead of connecting
to the I AM and Oneness.

I can look for
but not touch
the Prime Life Force.

Angels and guides
strip me divinely naked.

After the Rain Returns

Long-delayed rain has arrived.
It is more fun to meditate in the backyard
when it is warmer and sunnier.

I'd better not sit under a tree.
Heavier winds might plop raindrops on me
even after the storm has passed.

Branches on peach, pear, cherry,
apple and hazelnut trees have sprouted green fuzz
beside the gray-green crusty scabs.

Rain polka-dotted a three-leaf clover
and dotted blades of grass
to glisten even in muted light.

Our summer-tanned lawn has increased its green factor.
Leaf-curls nestle, dried-out grass revives.
Weeds thrive in the garden.

Unnecessary, coiled, green hose
curls on concrete. Nozzle–
the head of a slumbering snake.

Newly-built storage shed
has not been loaded with white plastic buckets,
gardening tools and crumpled small pool.

Noise from my neighbor's chainsaw
disturbs any attempts at concentration.
My attention is drawn outward.

I am having more fun
observing what is outside of me
than contemplating what is latent within me.

Revenant

Fall's grayed sky has relapsed
into a sunny, summery day
lightening the backyard.

In childhood I would have conjured fairies
flitting and scrambling in trees and bushes
instead of jays and squirrels.

Garden's blooms and holes held shelter for elves,
the castles in the sandbox terra-formed
into a whimsical landscape.

This shriveling garden's harvest is gone.
Leaf-cradles rock on withered flowerbed.
Stalks droop, not strut.

When I approach the backdoor,
it had locked behind me. I walk around the house
to find the front door locked.

Before I fumble for my keys, I see red holly berries.
How I wish I could see fairies nibbling them!
My inner child yearns to open the door.

Cover-ups in Cloudy Light

Gray clouds roll in portending predicted rain.
In un-shrouded intensity, sun
plays peek-a-boo with rushing clouds,
radiates then darkles.

I head for our newly-built backyard shed
where I store a blue camp chair.
I retrieve the folded chair stalked against beige wall
amid lawn gear and boxed wrapped apples.
Whiffs of new plastic waft to brisk breeze.

Planting the open chair
I prepare to absorb Gaia's energy—
chi through the feet,
stardust from the cosmos.

Plunked, scaly, windfall apples
cluster around the chair.
I adjust my red cape
over my exposed knees.
Short nightgown crumbles
angels and stars print.

Last surviving red gladiola blooms
remains hidden from view
behind cherry tree trunk.
A lone bee scurries nearby,
rustles in grass and curled leaves
then flies away.

Facing in and out sun,
hunkered behind clouds,
rays emerge to glow in cloud flow.
Sun perched above neighbor's roof-line
flickers like strobe-light enlightenment.

A massive gray cloud passes.
A pocket of sunlight radiates through,
but I am chilled as breezes sneak
under my cape behind my bent knees.

I head inside to warm,
hope my feet absorbed some chi.
As cosmic light obscures,
my vision shutter.

Juggling water bottle and open chair
I fumble toward the shed,
cape blowing in breeze.

Chair folds up and leans against wall.
Door closes without lock or key.
My conjurer's cape cloaks my covert operations
for connection on this clouding day.

Dampened Spirits

Moistened after two hours in the pool
I carry a blue camp chair
into the dimmed backyard.

I am still wet behind the ears
in my attempts to meditate
so I will contemplate what appears.

Gray clouds crowd.
grass still damp from early morning rain.
My red cape cocoons from chill.

Each morning I position the chair
in a different spot
for shifting viewpoints.

Solo gladiola blasts its last red bloom.
Remnant rose blushes blanched tips.
Closed dandelion dot snakes toward me like a cobra.

Garden devas must appreciate rain's assist
after weeks of sun-cracking clay,
roots seeking water, blooms beaming toward light.

Distant din of birdcalls,
drone of traffic–
unseen sound lulls me.

Plucked from chair pocket,
water bottle re-hydrates me.
I relax and rest my eyes.

When I open my eyes
through a gap of bush hedge, a peephole
to spy splash of purple blooms next door.

Chilled, dampened
I lug the chair across the lawn
to leave in the storage shed.

Gray hovers. Heavy air.
How I thirst for color
to breathe dry heat.

Barking Up The Wrong Tree

My acupuncturist suggests
I could conduce wood energy
if I put my bare foot against
the bark of a tree trunk.
She demonstrates placing
her bare foot against the smooth-sided
white massage table leg.
Similarly, in the pool
I stretch my calves against
concrete pool side in swim shoes.

I would try this against bark but—
I am diabetic. I should not
go barefoot and risk foot injury.
She says leather soles work best but—
the soles of my shoes are rubber
which insulates me from lightning strikes
and from absorbing Gaia's chi.

Surveying the most accessible trees
I discover bark has different textures.
Some have more loped limbs, knots and whorls.
Cherry bark rings horizontally
with oval dots running like Morse Code.
Filbert's trunk ripples smoothly to the ground,
river-teeth of moss and lichen patches.
Apple bark is scaly, vertical rivulets
cushioned by moss at the base.
Does moss create a barrier or soft cushioning?
The towering evergreen is much too rough
for stocking feet, a scratchy conduit.
Besides rain lingers on the grass
to dampen my heels. No sap in these socks.

She says the idea may be a little woo-woo anyway.
I spot the mossy sidewalk chunks
creating garden walls.
What about rock energy?
On a sunny day the rocky mini-plateaus
could warm and twitch toes,
prance and dance my feet.
I could greet sunrise in hole-ly socks
extending my arms to cosmic rays
or be a lazy dog lifting leg toward tree
and not touching.

Emanations

*Every artifact, every natural object ,with its ghostly wrappings or
associations and meanings, begotten and forgotten, is a gathering of minds
or contending voices, every thing is an invisible assembly. Robert Pinsky*

My red cape contends with my quagmire of quarks.
Hovering cape connects me
with shriveled red remnant gladiola
bent bloom sheath arcing in autumnal air.

Leaves curl and cover lawn reviving with rain
from arid summer, layering for winter.
Windfall apples collected and wrapped in newspaper–
with their worms, scales, bruises. packed away.

Recent neighbor pounds replacement slats in our back fence
recalls former neighbors who lived in that house.
We knew them better
and repaired the wood fence together.

All the particles swirling in the moist wind, arriving in mizzle,
churn, combine sparks of life.
Auras, shades, ghostly palimpsests from other dimensions,
determined star dust descendants create our destinies.

So much unknown, unseen, untouched, unheard.
So much begotten we have forgotten. Clutch what you can.
Backyard thoughts drift up front in my mind.
Warm elusive memories swarm as I hug cape snug.

Overcasting

On an overcast October morning
I sit on a blue camp chair
hands tucked under my red cape.

New wood or repaired slats
glare beside weathered gray fence
draw my attention to lighter places.

Buds no longer bloom.
Fewer windfall apples.
Leaves raked.

Only lavender puffs of clover
amid chunks of sidewalk wall.
No berries on the vines.

I overcast stitches of light
over my gloomy hem of grief–
mend, heal.

Warm hands on lap,
no longer sewing,
I free myself for prayer.

Dawning Light

Orange sunrise splays rays
between open spaces
of bushes in backyard hedge.

Neighbor's wooden fence
stakes a boundary
nearer our houses.

But our backyards butt
garden to garden
in orderly harmony.

Weeds remain a chaotic remnant
in the harvested areas
wildly, flagrantly errant.

I am a weed
as yellowing rays tamp
the butch-cut lawn.

Cinqueries

Women Poets

Maya Angelou

Life
masks dark
disguises.
Writhe light rhythms
free.

Adelaide Crapsey

Gray
garbed, wrote
lead cinquains.
Did not live 'til
gray.

Anne Sexton

Red
dress flares.
Poems inflame
passion while pain
burns.

May Swenson

Words
wriggle
in lines. Page
palette draws us
in.

Emily Dickinson

White
recluse
bridles thoughts—
circumference
wide.

Sylvia Plath

Bell
jar falls.
Oven chills
feverish, hot
pen.

Hazel Hall

She
hems, pens,
stitches life
in fabric, on
page.

Edna St. Vincent Millay

Flame
flickers
when candle's
wicks burn at both
ends.

Penny Avila

Loud,
shining
Penny. Our
poet beyond
cost.

The Written Word

When
lost in
words with muse
in another world,
I
connect
dimensions,
realities
in
my
thoughts to
make these worlds
possible and
real.

Pre-Writing

When
feelings
fall lower
to underground–
lift.

When
feelings
rise higher–
celestial--
cling.

When
feelings
within reach,
they can flow on
page.

Do
feelings
flow on page
when blocked by some
pain?

Low Life

Slugs
lasso
silver loops
on green targets;
grass.

Worms
puddled
on sidewalk
drowned in concrete
pool.

Ants
marching
to work, the
beat beneath my
feet.

Web
too low
to slow bugs.
Low, slow bugs are
feast.

Dew's
rainbow
freckles shine
to speckle our
day.

Mud
sucks rain,
slurps sun, thirst
parches, muddies
face.

Seeds
split, jut
stalks, spread roots,
tingling, tickling
earth.

Road
smothers
earth. Black, flat
murderer of
seed.

Orts

Orts
are crumbs
beneath the
table. We have
orts.

Ort
tofu,
ort crackers,
scrambled eggs, cheese,
chips.

Ort
apple,
yeast flakes, toast,
yogurt dollops,
snacks.

Ort
popcorn,
blueberries'
split skins oozing
goo.

Orts
return
each meal. They're
recyclable
orts.

Ort
bumps dash
color on
monotoned flat
rugs.

Ort
clutches.
grovels floor,
wants to remain
ort.

Ought
orts stay
for mice, bugs,
spiders? Good-bye
orts?

Soon
sucked in
bag, other
creatures mourn lost
orts.

I
miss
those
whose drops made
possible those
orts.

27

Light on Things

Cosmic Origins

Are
we star
dust? Comet
deposits? Now
us?

Bonding Dreams

Bond
with love.
Create light.
Rainbow spectrum
bright.

Radiant Energy

Light
beaming
increases
frequency of
hope.

Rainbow Reversal

Our
rainbow
arc-frown turns
upside down to
smile.

Dream Flights

Birds
feather
our light dreams;
carry our bright
hopes.

Light-Bearer's Lament

Light
in dark
places needs
clarity to
shine.

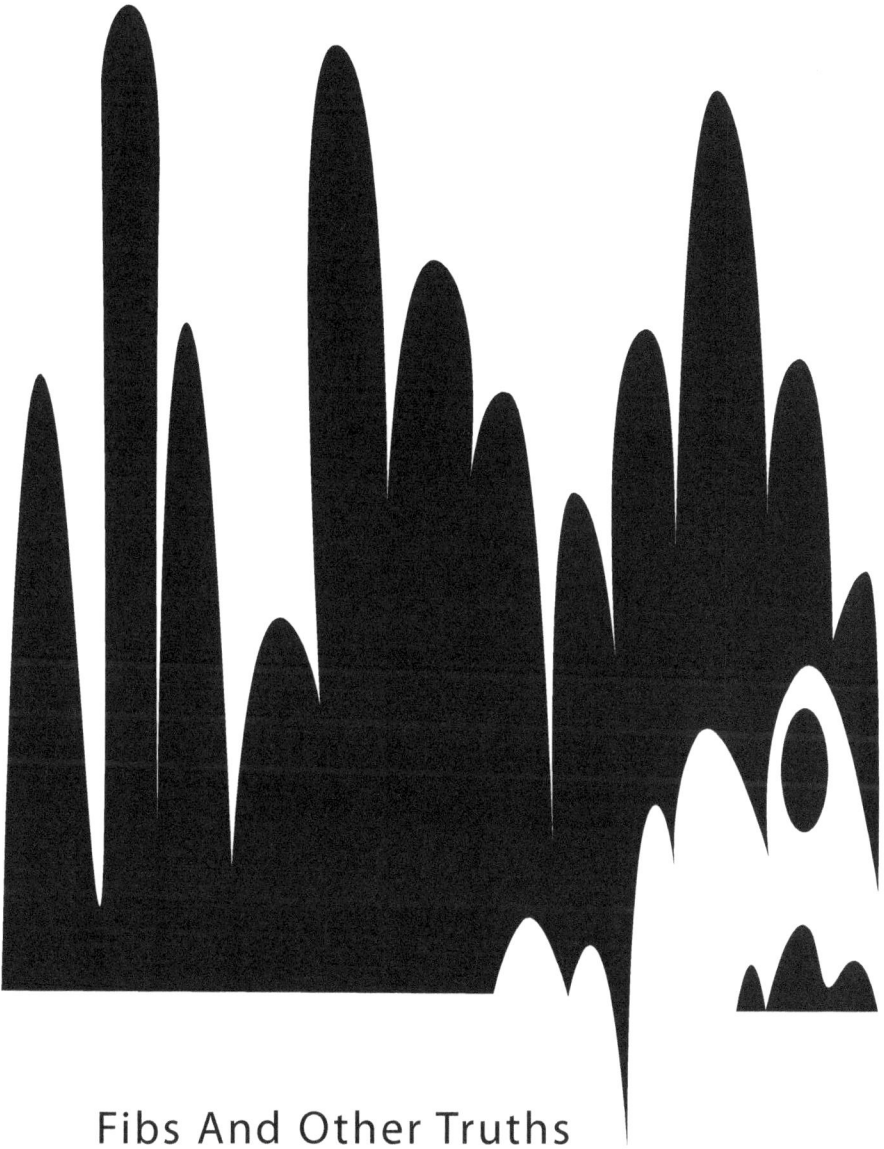

Fibs And Other Truths

Performances

Robert Frost in Connecticut

At
a chapel
white legend
read, then became drunk
with college fraternity boys.

May Swenson in New York City

She
read
at Y.
Bill Stafford
thought I came to see
him, but it was my mentor, May.

Martha Graham on Broadway

Draped
in shroud
she unfurls,
opens her darkness,
dances to final curtain call.

Taylor Mali at National Poetry Slam
at Wesleyan in Connecticut

My
first
slam rocks
with his voice,
articulation,
clear tone with gestures, muscled words.

Billy Collins in Portland, Oregon

He
was
so proud
of the crowd,
he tossed the questions
to the floor, dismissing his fans.

Lawson Fusao Inada
Oregon Poet Laureate
Portland, Oregon

His
wide
smile which
opens laughs,
explodes poetry
with playful, practical actions.

Carolyn Forche in Corvallis, Oregon

When
she
read "The
Colonel " I
discovered prose poems.
Students' watered ears listening.

Maya Angelou in Corvallis, Oregon

She
sings,
dances,
reads her poems,
so stately, strong, proud.
Phenomenal woman struts stuff.

31

Yusef Komunyakaa in Corvallis, Oregon

Blues,
jazz,
surreal,
bear witness,
"pulsates with psyche."
Gray shirt, gray vest, silver rings, hair.

William Stafford
Haystack Workshop in Oregon

At
coast
workshop
he posts poems
with all the others,
centering student's poetry.

Stephen Hawking in Portland, Oregon

Scrunched
in
wheel chair,
fingers spell,
communicate words
for his voice synthesizer speech.

Vast
mind
explores
universe.
He types. Limited
movements for unlimiting mind.

Scissor Steps

Her
steps
scissor
from home down
blank sidewalk sheets toward
kindergarten. She hugs a dog,

plucks
green
leaves to
brown and curl,
carefully traces
puddle edges, stumbles on root.

Blood
snakes
down leg.
Handkerchief
traps blood snake to worm.
Bandaid tunnels hidden blemish.

My
hand
cradles
hers until
she sees her new friend.
Her hand hinges with hers, swinging.

Legs
skip
to the
classroom door.
She blends as bandage
into her room, to cut and draw.

Summer Girl

As
a
free-borne
butterfly
fluttering in sky,
she wings her skirt and flower-flits.

She
will
gather
dew, skirting
transient nectar
of these golden gossamer hours.

Soon
she'll
cocoon
her wide skirts,
curtail whirling flight.
Fall comes for her. Too soon. Too soon.

Dreamer

On
his
copied
papers he
doodles airplane flight
which the teacher marks, "messy".

On
his
cover
(standardized
text), he scribbles joke
which humorless teacher rips off.

On
desk
(metal,
formica)
he crayoned his name
which the neat teacher wiped away.

On
the
window's
transparent
sheet, he sketches dreams
which unheard teacher could not see.

When Expectation Is Round

He
was
waiting
for her at
noon, his mind licking
lollipops, lemon drops by pounds.

At
one
crumpled
hope strewn,
his angel cake flops, his
cookie jar now is gobbled down.

At
six
spinach
on plastic
spoon, not hungry he
then hops after a ball he found.

She
is
a popped
balloon whose
string drops worm-like to
melted chocolate candy ground.

First Snowfall

A
boy
near by
makes snow fly,
angles it, packs it,
to fortify, spins it, smacks sky.

From
my
window
his lawn greens.
He ambles over.
"Can I borrow some of your snow?"

Flower Seller in Long Beach

stands
on
corner
holding a
flower to his nose,
granny glasses, barefoot, haunting.

Long
hair
Christ-like,
flower child
in a concrete garden.
He swivels stem and sniffs the bloom.

Eyes
on
own world,
hunched, almost
monastically frail,
alone, he holds flower like grail.

Changeable Plates

We
used
paper
plates for kids
when small; can break them.
Disposable after they're used.

It
was
handy,
colorful
for celebrations,
coordinates with themes.

No
fear
breaking
tableware.
Matches with the cups.
Napkins patch beside plate like quilt.

Now
we're
older,
break inside,
risk breakable wares,
use ancestral fragile plates.

I
learned
to use
beautiful,
irreplaceable
dishes–precious–like who use them.

Raccoon Zoo Food

Wad
of
bubble
gum pimples
the concrete. Raccoon
paws possible feast. Sinewy
strings
are
shaped so
dextrously
from spaghetti to
meatball before raccoon escapes.

At Too Many Meetings

Coughs
clutch
the air
and whispers
vibrate stagnant sounds
from podiums as toes stab socks.

Legs
clap
thighs, arms
cross dueling
swords, while marbled eyes,
habit smiles and un-shook hands wait.

Chaired
for
silence,
boxed-down brains
rarely stand up. My
hungry tongue a buttered knife.

Slice
the
table
talk, idle
coated words. Request
portion for unserved waiting.

White Socks on the Line

Like
teeth
they hang.
Holes await
fillings. Their bracing
clothes-pins hold line to gnaw the gale.

Mud-
hands
make spots-
cavities-
extract them from line,
leaves gum-smile under scowling sky.

A Sun-glassed World

Tint
your
world view.
Nothing so
glaring. Asphalt
black-lashing earth. Poles string charged line.

Oil
clots
catching
shore life in
spreading sore, stolid
buildings watch like grounded gray gulls.

Fish
face
gravish
scrub board dams.
Smoke bleaches the sky.
White-washed fabric, dotted people.

World
hues
hidden.
Daubs of death
dilute rainbow thoughts
as colors fade. Sun-glassed world waits.

A Tactile-less Slug

A
slug
left his
bristly, butch
cut, verdure forest
for emerald, house wall desert.

Gray
arcs—
loopy
glistenous,
oil-puddly hues—
ooze from this color-sighted slug,

as
he
re-tracks
to bark dust,
gladiolas, grass
in his endless hunger for green.

Birds at McDonald's

Birds
perch
on the
drooping limbs
of golden M, flit
tile roof to litter cans, nibble
bits
of
buns on
tables, on
asphalt and concrete.
Birds feast on worm-like french fried treats.
Pie,
shakes,
burger
bites stick beak and feet.
Paper crumbs neighborhood.
Birds ignore bark dust with flower chunks.
M
frowns
on the
window like
tired wings, as birds
fly from these texture-less trees.

Sidewalks

They
paved
flowers
and grass, but
boots not concrete keep
feet dry. Walk worn paths to neighbors.
Earth=
feet,
asphalt=
wheels. Direct
paths follow people
but sidewalks follow the street.

Lid
for
life and
for movement,
swaying blades gone for
skipping feet. Small life dies. Bigger
forms
can
now move
faster. But
on sluggish paths, life
touches life. Mud hugs. Grass tickles.

Telephone Pole Crosses

Head
stone
crosses,
graveyard sky,
stripped, uprooted, stab
paved earth. Wired words pole to pole.

A
staff,
note-less,
sustains birds
sporadic songs on
skeletons of singing forests.

With
nails
still in
double cross
crucifixes, we
make crosses in air and in earth.

Un-bandaged World

I
long
to look
at sunset--
no wires, scratches;
see sun un-gauzed with filmy air.

To
feel
the earth
unbound and
tickly, in a world–
un-bandaged and whose wounds have healed.

Chips Off the Old Block

Blocks
cut
corners,
chisel, roll,
un-squared, weakened, they're
sculpted at end—hollow zero.

A Snapshot Thought

When
life
flicks fast
as movie,
some wish a slide show
but not photo locked in album.

An Envelope

knows
what's
within.
Flap—snoopy
nose—points toward taut
square chin. But has no ears, no eyes,
no
lips.
It's sealed
surface hides,
privately conceals
surprise. We are licked by a stamp.

A Pebble

If
I'm
destined
to be but
a pebble in world,
throw me into a pool. Wavelets
can
grow
to shore.
Lake or sea
I make no contact
as I sink to the bottom. Since
I
am
not a
rock, boulder–
give me a pool, for
I'd like to feel I've touched somewhere.

Black Stars on a White Sky

* Black Star on a White Sky

We are the hollow men
We are the hollow men
Leaning together
Headpiece filled with ink, Alas!

Rick the asterisk had another migraine
from all the constant clatter.
He was placed above the well-used dash
on the typebar.
To the typist it did not matter
that ink caked his unused limbs.
Thickened and listless from lack of exercise
he looked around at the other characters,
quiet and meaningless after extensive use.
He was pushed and pounded too
but his imprint was never on the page–
always the dash. He was a fading star.
He felt like a hammer and anvil at once.
His migraine was just nerves
from his sense of uselessness.

Perhaps he could imprint himself on the page.
If imbedded deep enough...they couldn't erase.
Just think, on the page at last–
guiding people to important ideas.
This fading, flatulent star would twinkle as
a dynamic not dying star.
He cartwheeled
        spun the rollers
                chinned the bar.
He paused to ponder the print–
quotes from T.S. Eliot's "The Hollow Men".
Such strange patterns of darkness on light.
Where would he fit in?
He roamed letter by letter down the first line.

Risk roller-coastered over the **W**
and peeked through the **e**.
He pulled the **a**'s tail.
He used the **r** as an arm rest.
When he reached the second **e**
        he played leapfrog on his bent back.
He played scarecrow with the **t** but found
        he had extra arms to dangle
        over the crossbar.
He drooped on the **h**'s hump.
He massaged another aching **e**
        who was very round-shouldered.
When he reached the next **h**
        he sat down and thought.
Many letters needed his assistance. The **o**
        was dizzy in that position
The two **ll**'s found proximity a problem.
Risk tried to pacify arguments.
The next **o** felt caged in.
Risk opened him for a stretch.
The **w** felt bottom heavy
The **m** felt top heavy, so they switched
        positions for awhile.
The **e** wanted to be a capital E.
Risk explained his importance
in the scheme of things.
The line ended with the **n**.
n was well-rounded and stood solidly
on his own two feet. He bent
with demands yet was flexible.
n urged Risk who was free to move on
to help the other letters on the page.
They were all printed
and had responsibilities to stay in their places.
There was no period at the end of the line.

Yes, Risk would make a shift in his freedom.
He would not embed but provide others
with marginal release.
He would be his own justifier.
Cheerfully, Risk moved
      letter by letter
        word by word
          sentence by sentence
            row by row.

Untangling double f's,
giving diet encouragement to p's and q's and d's,
subtly giving v's and s's a lesson in humility,
applauding the forward looking ideas of the k's,
prodding the sullen g's to be friendly
with the jolly j's.
The c's were depressed.
The u's were envious of the w's extra space.
Often only a kind or well-timed word,
a new insight, a gentle touch
was all that was needed.
They were so engrossed
in their own impressions,
they failed to see how they blended
with their neighbors.
They needed to realize their utility
as a group as well as their individuality.
Perhaps if they shared a typehead
like he did before being printed
(the numbers and punctuation marks
seemed to be better adjusted characters)
or if they were cursive type
and connected more,
more good feeling would flow between them,
Anyway, he tried.

When Risk finished his rounds,
he walked tightropishly up to the typehead,
careful not to fall in the typewriter's grooves–
hollow valleys for dying stars.
He climbed to the top of the dash just in time.
The metal images were raised
receiving supplication of the man's hand
under the twinkle of a fading star.
The sheet rolled out. A new sheet rolled in.

Risk was no longer on the page,
but he had made an imprint.
He smiled and chanted as the roller turned.
        "Here we go round the prickly pear
        Prickly pear, prickly pear
        Here we go round the prickly pear
        At five o'clock in the morning."
He sobered as he remembered another verse–
        "This the way the world ends
        This is the way the world ends
        This is the way the world ends
        Not with a bang but a whimper."

Risk would go on to other pages other days.
He would continue to bang not whimper...always.

* He did. Risk became Eliot's perpetual star...
The hope of empty men.

Asterisking

An asterisk animates.
A radiating star,
an asteroidal starfish,
a dandelion puff,
an aster head
petalling on the page.
The tumbleweed symbol
indicates omissions,
a reference mark to keep writers on track,
alerting us to a hypothetical,
nonoccuring linguistic form.
Three pyramidal asterisks
draw attention to a passage.
As I funnel letters
onto an asteriskless sheet
I try not to disasterisk
as words roll into lines,
radial with centered thoughts.
I asterisk constellations
and hopefully ray
my reflected light asterisms
into asteriated eyes.

*
* *

Suprapoeming

I'll start to prepoem
a sort of wannabe poem;
discover a propoem
not a prose or con poem.
Will it become a be poem,
a me, he or shepoem?
A hit or mispoem?
A yes or dispoem?

A malpoem is easy.
A surpoem is breezy.
A subpoem needs a lift.
A contrapoem breaks a rift.
A repoem has been done before.
A depoem became prose once more.
An enpoem after revisions
reveals a propoem with excisions.
An extrapoem must reduce.
A transpoem must travel loose.

Maybe an interpoem or intropoem,
a monopoem or retropoem?
No claustropoem but obpoem.
Not pseudopoem or antipoem
but a telepoem or dynapoem.
Maybe a macropoem or micropoem,
megapoem, megalapoem?

A superpoem with sound, sense and sight,
an ultrapoem of undulating delight
would be such an in or onpoem—
one to pounce upon poem.

I seek the multipoem,
a high difficulty poem.
But I have not even a quasipoem,
a semi, demi, hemipoem.

I must repoem the unpoem.
I must compoem the nonpoem.

A poemphile enpoems, colpoems,
autopoems, morphpoems, epipoems,
abpoems, acpoems, adpoems,
biopoems, peripoems, perpoems,
synpoems, sympoems, sylpoems,
polypoems until postpoem—
        a benepoem
        an archpoem
        the suprapoem.

Fairies Can Fly Because
They Make Themselves Lightly

Contemporary fairies are a-flutter,
not sure how to wing-it in the New Age.
Shape-shifters trapped in myth–
how do you fly away when hinged
to open-winged pages of outdated books?

Fairies are running out of habitat
for mushroom roofs, flower umbrellas,
meadows for dance circles.
Mound cities are plowed into subdivisions.
Fairies dig deeper into caverns, caves
with entries too small for people.
Some plan to hole out in depleted mines.

Pollution nibbles fairy wings lacy.
Fairies steal cellophane and clear
contact paper for repairs.
When they shift density, they find
particulate deposits tumor their bodies.

Gossamer gowns and tights are gone.
Soft, thin duds could not handle
the rough edges of the modern world.
Some switched to plastic jeans or
armored from decay with aluminum foil
unisex jump-suits. The glare blinds them.

Long tresses tangle in wires,
cables, antennae, poles. Hair no longer
combs in flexible limbs of clear-cut trees.
Those not bald from chemical fallout
wear close-shaven hair.

Their former food foysom
without additives now requires them to be
hunters and gatherers of the essence
of organic gardens where they alight
on vacation from their dark domiciles.

Their communication wave-length was jammed
by e-mail and the Internet. They had to re-tune
their vibrations to a higher level
to frequencies governments couldn't sell out.
Their inner light dims with film of grime
like headlights in a mud-slinging storm.

As their popularity diminished,
fairies consulted with angels,
currently on a faddish high.
At a Wing Summit on a cumulus cloud,
fairies asked their celestial cousins
if the universe had another realm
for such adaptable, light-bearing beings.
The luminous angels said
to their dimmed fallen comrades
"Lighten up."

Fairies rid themselves. of baggage,
radiation bringing darkness
not light, shades to their light.
With fairy flare they tossed ghostly garb.
Bareheaded, tattooed nudes fly with recycled
feather-patched wings flicking detritus
of deteriorating civilization.
After bathing in purifying pools,
unclogged bells tinkle.
Inner-light flashlight recharging
lanterns of light, give all a lift.

Above the ozone layer
in their new simply abundant lofts,
some take a powder with stardust,
hitchhike on a satellite,
bop like hail with a comet,
or sing-along with angels.

Cosmic changelings, endangered Earthlings,
fairies can fly on because they make
themselves lightly. When they descend to our digs,
they travel light on this heavy planet.

Shiny Roots*

Supposedly
    Adam and Eve
    and other fertile pairs
    seeded Earthlings with moist encounters.

    Spaceships of Lyrans
    and Mardukans,
    Pleiades and Sirius volunteers
    planted stardust descendants.

    Early people's creation myths
    used mud and clay,
    sweat from giant armpits;
    spilled cosmic eggs
    to evoke yolky-folk.

    Quirky couplings
    of primordial pairs,
    star stuff
    mud pies
    thought forms
    started DNA spirals
    into people.
    Smaller eggs and mini-sperm
    bulb into bodies
    of questionable origin.

Maybe
       we are solidified thought
       made flesh,
       magically touched
       by stardust.

       The universe sent
       its best ideas
       And experiments
       to play here.
       On high they watch us
       and wonder if we have shiny roots
       for we are their plants
       they have transplanted so often.

* Plants develop shiny roots when transplanted too many times.

Reading Swedish Poets

Pages splay face to face.
Swedish on the left.
English on the right.
Horizontal colons
or vertical halos
hover over Swedish a's and o's.
I do not know their names or sounds.
I can't find the symbols
on my computer.
So I can't spell Edith Sodergran,
Gunnar Ekelof or Tomas Transtromer
in a Swedish way.
Harry Martinson is without rounded spots.
A guide book assures me
Swedish vowels have only one sound
but does not name the symbols.
A friend says the sounds
oh, aah, eh in ways I can't pronounce.
The language of my grandparents
is foreign to me.
I can't translate side to side
and correspond words directly to meaning.
This summer when I visit Sweden
and walk ancestral ground
with the gist of poet relative
Sven Vallare's chapbook
translated for me
I hope these relatives
know English if they read my poetry.
Without hovering symbols
my lines lie flat on the page.

Sharing Lord Byron
        for Clara Swenson Varsell

Grandma's 1848 *Works of Lord Byron*
sent to me after her death
was found in her attic
wrapped in black satin covered cardboard.
The glue, rust-like on the spine
was not binding.
Beige shadows of the etchings,
old newspaper clippings
and age spots blotch pages.
Near the beginning
her clipping of robed young Byron.
Near the middle
Lady Byron's Answer to Lord Byron's "Farewell".
A yellowed ribbon over fading, tiny type
marks Grandma's place.

The years we lived closely
we talked about history.
The years we lived apart
we wrote about family,
not knowing we shared poetry.
I turn fragile pages.
Now sharing Lord Byron
Grandma seems as unknown
as the raggedly cut
sepia-ed clip
of a woman with 1920 hair
tucked near the end of the book
beside the verse
"Nothing so difficult as a beginning in poesy
unless perhaps the end."

A Perfect Excellent Lovely Sunflower Existence
Allen Ginsberg

For Helen Erickson Varsell

My mother collects sunflowers.
She plants them around all her rooms
in pots, on cups, place mats, dolls.
Showers of yellow petals. Sunshine blooms.
But on the phone she asks me why?

Why sunflowers? I read Ginsberg.
Sunflower Sutra puzzles her.
Ode to nature? Pollution dirge?
Poetry saves grime-faced flower.
She brightens life, twinkle in eye.

We're all golden sunflowers inside
Allen Ginsberg

It's the Cherries, Stellar Jays

Those blue-breasted, blue-headed birds are back
chomping on all our almost-ripe cherries.
The cat's having another snooze attack.
Someone must save our pink, pubescent berries.
The professor in his going-to-campus clothes
with tall ladder he will thwart these foes.

Chomping on all our almost ripe cherries,
Stellar Jays squawk with glee as they flee.
We approach to stake our ladder with ease
against the bird-pecked, people-picked tree.
Uneven ground makes Professor's step unstable
but he grabs hard-fleshed cherries for our table.

The cat's having another snooze attack.
That lolling in the sun, sprawling, lollygagging cat
hears me bird-booing and without looking back
lollops from the yard. Prof really doesn't like that
"useless, flea-bitten, barfing, bird-watching creature.
You don"t have any redeeming feature!"

Someone must save our pink, pubescent berries
so Professor with me as his stabilizing force
conquers the ladder, reclaims his cherished cherries
while at the bottom I check our cherry resource.
My fingers nibble low-branch berries to a bowl
before bothersome birds extract their toll.

The professor in his going-to-campus clothes–
vest flapping like a robbing bird's wings–
his hands pluck and peck until he slows.
The rickety ladder sways and swings.
He curses the cat and his lack of time
to salvage his harvest, to prevent this crime.

With tall ladder he will thwart these foes.
Down he struts with bowl cherry-bellied high–
smile-puffed cheeks all cherry-pink glows.
As he carries cherries indoors with a sigh,
the professor knows as soon as he is out of sight
those blues-bringing birds will feast day and night.

Little Man with a Spade

Grandpa may be at times
the man with the hoe.
James at any opportunity
is the little man with a spade.
Both like to dig,
tussle with the earth,
fling it and make it breathe.
They select shovels
in different sizes
for earth- moving.
At the playground
pebbles bounce like hailstones
off flattened surfaces.

No weed is safe
when the pointy trowel
prowls the roots of an intruder.
Side-by-side they dig–
glint for upheaval in their eyes.
Plastic equipment is for sand.
These guys relish the rusty patina
of dirty, grimy metal
with wooden handles.
Side-by-side they spy for spots
to thrust their tools
and toss to abandon.

They look for large yellow diggers
dribbling crumbling firmament
into dump truck,
or waiting motionless
gathering raindrops
in the gobbling mud.
Watching or digging
Grandpa and James
love to see weeds and dirt fly.
They need to pitch in–
shifting the weight of the world around.

James in the Garden

In the hard, cracked dirt
of the droopy, desiccated garden,
James with his Oshkosh overalls
and Pooh shirt
carried his encrusted shovel to dig
with a swish and a flourish
until distracted by butterflies,
he decides to try
to blow bubbles which
glow hollow, rainbowed spheres
over the withered ground
just waiting for moisture
in the hot sun, where
the peaked grass
mowed in uniform blandness
bluntly watches as James
joyously stomps bubbles
into their monotonous midst or
triumphantly tosses burping bubbles
over the fence into dry air.

We Climb a Hill For Kip

We climb a fog-bound hill,
await the muted sunrise
filtering through the fog.
We bring
beloved ashes
to share life here.
At daybreak
his hand-thrown ashes
are sown on the moist hillside
near a young tree about his age.
My mothering hand
which caressed his flesh
cannot handle his ashes.

Gray ash blurs in the misty air.
Ashes like fog settle on grass
and earth to nourish life.
Fog softly tamps the ashes to the ground.
We long to feel the warmth of sun.

We climb the cloudy hill
await the hidden sun.
His ashes are gone.
Rain buries him.
He remains forever nineteen.

If only the pain would fall
as gently as the rain,
would lift as the sun
lifts the dew on the hillside.

In Suspended Animation

I am part of this mobile
with its suspended bodies
orbiting on taut strings.

Captive of currents
I ponder you as gently
I blow you into spasmodic jerking.

It is not easy to turn in new directions
by moving slowly, smoothly,
undisturbed, resting on a string.

Both of us precariously balanced,
each part alone in a pattern.
Forcefully I blow again.

The driven bodies dance–
leaping, twirling, touching...tangling.
One falls...then all.

Most revolutions begin and hope to end
as an act of liberation
...for all.

I let the mobile lie–
detached, unmoved, unstrung.
I cannot create a new design.

But someone will re-string us.
Someone will restore our orbit.
Then someone will breathe freedom.

Interview with a Dream Programmer

Welcome to Seven Star Dream Enterprises,
the Dream Distribution Service of Choice.
I am your personal dream programmer
for this evening. Thank you for choosing us.
By answering the following questions
I can program the dream that best fits your needs.
Do you prefer retro black and white
or technicolor?
Would you like a therapeutic dream?
Or a vivid contact dream?
Conscious dreaming
or dreaming to transform reality?
Do you want an in-body
or out-of-body experience?
Do you want to revisit past lives?
Specify time period and planet.
Explore different dimensions? Celestial touring?
Peek into parallel lives?
View another person's dreams?
How about a stimulating sex dream?
Somnolent serenity?
Sleep walk for exercise?
Snoring or talking accompaniment?
Exam preparation with recall?
Preview or review multitudinous media options?
Do you need help with dream interpretation
or symbology?
Warnings for your exit points? Premonitions?
Clairvoyant information on future choices?
Look into some reality checks? Surreality?
Try distant viewing and visit
someone alive or dead?
Do you want to dream with people
in your current reality?
Or strangers in another dimension or time?
Do you want to retain your experiences,
insights and ideas when awake?

We have a special offer
on action-packed adventures? Horror flicks?
We monitor them for adrenalin rushes
and provide safety nets for falling dreams.
You cannot transit from an encounter
in a containerized cosmos.
How about a creative dream?
A connection with your muse?
Chat with your guardian angel?
We don't get many requests for nightmares,
but they can be arranged.
Or we provide nightmare eraser?
Stress reduction techniques? Blissful music?
Problem solving solutions? Inventive ideas?
How long do you want to dream?
Do you want multiple choices?

Sorry to interrupt your dream state
but you are not responding.
We want to know the quality of our programming.
Do you want me to transfer you to customer service?
We do have quotas and bonuses
so please do not wake up on me until I have finished
the questionnaire and programmed your responses.
Usually do your dream choices make you
refreshed or tired when waking?
What! You want a dreamless, good night's sleep
to recover from last night's choices?

The Land Octopus
        (Travelus Trailorus Vulgarus)

The land variety of octopus
is often glossy white as wet stones
with color fins on its sides.
Its blimpish body is headless.
Nerves wired in inner skin
conduct at the flip of a switch.
Its brain remains undetected.

Eyeless, vestigial transparent lids
are often curtained from sun and moon.
When led, there is no need to see.

Sucker bearing arms of the sea species
are specialized on land.
Sewage, water, electric lines,
leveling jacks, hitch, tires
tentacle to the ground and poles.
These tentacles do not coil to crunch,
but twirl rubbery tendrils
or shaft solidly straight.
They draw and discharge
to service others,
sporadically connect then
retract within.

Unlike the soft sea species,
it has a metalized shell
more like a crustacean.
Its awnings breathe air like gills.
Breezes wave over too low grass.
Black top lies too flat to touch its body.
Rain stripes road dirt,
rusts until the bulk is crushed away.

Its enlarged shape is to hold its prey.
The door mouths people in.
They churn inside its belly.
Tourists swallowed from the world
peer out its aperatures.
Land octopi cannot digest their prey.
They remain hollow.

Wantonly violated, they become
impregnated with people
who gestate in its metal womb
until birthed through its rigid opening.
Land octopi remain sterile.

Bulbous genitals hang near the hitch.
It mates with cars.
Hooked by cars for movement,
they migrate asphalt and concrete
searching for landings.
Cars command when to blink light.
Cars uncouple and roll away.

Land octopi park, never land.
Never root. Never firm a foundation.
Nestless, restless,
the earth flattens for them.

Poems That Count

Origins

Someone lit a spark,
ignited the dark,
made whole
celestial park,
infinity, quark,
black hole.

Before Eve's foot-mark,
death beneath flood-mark
formed coal.
Noah built an ark
loading first–aardvark
(then vole?)

In the air–skylark
In the sea–the shark
earth–mole.
On land–leaf, bud, bark,
shoal, knoll.

In our mind–remark
In our psyche-cark.
A soul
imagines a snark,
invents water-mark,
bead roll.

Universe's mark
creates lush from stark.
Extol!
Watch essence embark,
the pattern–endarch.
Loophole?

Road's Scholar

Oh give me a job without car
where I sit in office all day
with my own computer and play
and do not have to go far
feeling sick, tired, or under par.

Please, just let me work in one place
and avoid the traffic rat race.
Let me teach in only one room
and watch my rooted students bloom
without my mobile carapace.

Variations on Robert Frost

Trees Make Good Neighbors

Blue
spruce spires
heavenward,
blocks neighbor's yard
view.

When Two Paths Diverge in Woods

Two
paths fork
in forest—
either one, I'm
lost.

When I See Certain Trees

East—
birches.
West— aspens.
Beauty bends my
mind.

Stopping By Woods on Rainy Afternoon

Leaves
lovely,
damp and deep.
Hours to go to
dry.

Acquainted with Insomnia

Sleep
evades.
Stars and rain
don't drop my eyes–
books.

Ice and Fire

World
could freeze,
sun burn crisp,
universe suck
air.

Divide, Divide

Fame,
fortune,
friendship, love–
share with others,
give.

Grandma's Grandson's Grammar

Curled on
couch, he sleeps as
question mark. Awakens
to become exclamation point
or dash.

Alien Visitors

When aliens chose to land,
we met them with a band.
>　They were so surprised
>　the group they comprised
left. They couldn't understand.

When the aliens tried again,
polluted air gave them pain.
>　They began to wheeze
>　in the particulate breeze
and blew us away. No gain.

The aliens tried once more
to contact and to explore.
>　They received such a blast
>　they knew they wouldn't last
Such violence is hard to ignore.

You'd think the aliens gave up
(Their leaving was so abrupt)
>　but they stayed in their craft
>　thinking Earthlings are daft
then caused volcanoes to erupt.

The Earthlings watched the flow
and hovering aliens the glow
>　"We came to add light
>　not add to their plight,"
said an alien in the know.

When aliens tried to descend,
Earthlings just couldn't comprehend.
>　To prevent war
>　they left once more.
Cosmic visits came to an end.

Thinking of Columbine High

Rain
thuds on
windshield like
on bullet-proof
vest.

Safe
behind
windshield from
hard radio
talk.

Tears
roll as
the rain streaks
for pellets of
world.

Poems That Count Too

Becoming A Poet

Turns at Scrabble

Perhaps the way to go
with a B is to make BRO.
Then I am ready now
to add a letter for BROW.
The next letter I put down—
a beige tile-becomes BROWN.
Oh my brilliance is crowning.
I became a poet with BROWNING.

With Word Play

In China long ago
lived a poet Li PO.
Centuries later
American Edgar Allan POE.
Before you know it
I have created POET.
Being noetic
I become POETIC,
so hypothetically
I am thinking POETICALLY.

By Syllable Counts

A
verse
begins,
manifests
letter-by-letter—
unique characters down the line.

Poetry Caching in Spring

A realtor box
with free poems staked in yard
awaits visitors

Some walkers pick up
poems, thinking house for sale,
crumble, toss poems

Rain seeps in the box
dribbles down smudging pages.
Sun will curdle them

Walkers sit on wall
resting, reading poems, put
in backpacks or hands

Yanked up by the stake
to mow lawn, rests on trash can
near camelias

Hail pelts plastic
casing, white as snow, soft ping
droned out by traffic

Stick-on, raised letters
offer poetry to all
who come to pass by

Hallowing Ground For Kip

We climbed a fog-bound hill
carried our beloved son's ashes
to be buried by relentless rain.
Fog tamped ashes into moistened ground
until one day ashes were gone.
We yearned for warmth of sun.

Daily tears resurrect him. Sun
lifts the dew on the dampened hill.
Leaves shroud. Seeds cradle. Seasons gone.
An alder breeds from the ashes,
burrows roots in hardened ground
massaged by softening rain.

Can pain fall gently as rain
or joy lighten days as sun?
We tread hallowed ground.
Our recovery remains uphill.
Our hands cannot feel ashes
or caress flesh forever gone.

When laughter blooms, some numbness gone.
When grief tugs, memories rein.
Our lives, like fog blurred by ashes,
tendril toward renewing sun;
seek haven on his lofty hill
and hope not found on common ground.

Sow particles of life when death has ground
hearts to fragments, wholeness gone.
We clamber to clearing hill
across stones speckled with motes of rain.
We see dust in rays of sun
and remember hand-thrown ashes.

With warmth drawn from cooled ashes
we step for more solid ground.
Mist clears. We know our son
is with us always. Love's never gone.
Our grandson Haidan Regn's
placenta nourishes life on that hill.

On a tended hill we left ashes
tendered by rain on greyed ground
Heavy grief gone, lightened by sun.

New Aging

From
egg
and sperm
new being
begins to explore
life lessons on this hard planet.
One
loves
into
families,
generations pass.
One leaves what one dreams, understands.
When
I
must go,
joyfully,
what gifts can I leave?
My words, objects, love, memories?
I
think
my bliss
will go too.
Any remnant can
weave into a fabric of life.
So
take
what you
want to keep.
I'll be winging-it
and don't need earth-tugging luggage.

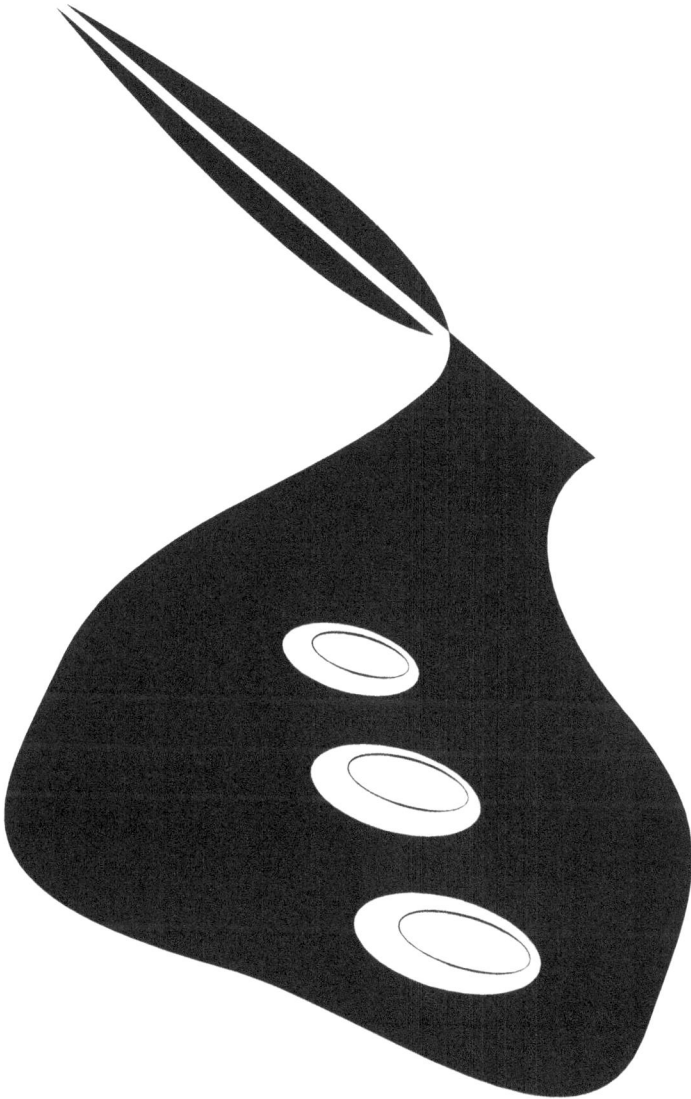

Syllables of Velvet

Childhood Prayers

My first prayers were in Swedish.
I mispronounced every word.
But I was certain my God heard.
Did not know meaning in English.

I did not understand the words
but I was fervent in spirit and intent.
I prayed unheard alone in my room.
Expectant, well-meaning, sought answers.
Over my head on slanted white wall
greenish stars glowed in the dark.

Though my prayers were out-loud shards,
sounds with strange symbols, gibberish,
later I wrote prayers not childish,
staffs like dedicated shepherds.

My laced fingers clutched shut,
no steeple pointed hands.
Prayers sprinkled like stardust
into the cosmos toward God.
In church I learned the Lord's Prayer
where people popped prayers like pills.

Gud some haver barnen kar (God who loves the children)
Se till meg som liten ar (watch over me who is little)

Thanksgiving at Grandma's

Grandma
burns pies,
roasts turkey dry.
Flecked
potatoes drool.
Crock smells.

Gravy
lumps.
We frown
at mangled food.
Not a scene like
Rockwell's.

Our First Thanksgiving Out of Grace

Empty armed chair at our table,
carry on as we are able,
try to eat. Our son's death starves us.
Flesh feeds our flesh, but not our soul.
Cut to pieces, stabbing our whole–
like a knife in breast, death carves us.
Empty armed chair at our table
carry on as we are able.

Never to return, daily trust.
Mourning our grace, we are hungry, thrust–
try to eat. Our son's death starves us.
Like a knife in breast, death carves us.
Empty armed chair at table,
carry on as we are able.

In Gardens of Earthly Delights

When you travel with vegetarians
you are uprooted at meals.
With the zeal of seminarians,
it's no blood, but what chops and peals.

You are uprooted at meals,
planted with new dietary seeds.
It's no blood, but what chops and peals
to meet your nutritional needs.

Planted with new dietary seeds
for your blooming body garden
to meet your nutritional needs
you have to ask their pardon.

When you travel with vegetarians
for your blooming body garden
with the zeal of a seminarian
you have to ask their pardon.

Nuyorican Poet's Café: My Cultural Icon

Poetry the vital sign of a new culture needed to be heard.
Miquel Algarin, Founder of the café in 1973

I dream of being in the Nuyorican Poet's Café–
venue of theater, film, spoken word, poetry slam.
Go over the Hudson River bridge of Long Island freeway
and you're also near hip hop, comedy, art, Latin Jazz, Jam.

I would fly to Boston, see family and friends
then head to the lower East Side–Alphabet City,
in the Big Apple where a sound bite never ends,
find the iconic café full of artistic creativity.

I'll take my fifth book of poetry along
but there's no slam poem in my repertoire,
so I'll take "Suprapoeming" my most strong
performing poem for my debut night noir.

I'll howl like yippee hound dog Arwen
after the poetry slam at the Open Room,
dramatically read my one poem, then
nurture my emergent slam poem to bloom.

I'll watch some hip hop, hear some jazz.
I can't dance. My knees say "Nevermore."
But I'll listen to poet's razz-a-ma-tazz
spotlighted with or without a judge or score.

I yearn to see this multi-cultural diversity
despite the crowd, rude staff and disgusting bathrooms.
It is a place for artists in New York City–
the café where ground-breaking work mushrooms.

I believe I can write a slam poem this year.
For poets this café is plenty of heaven.
I want to go there, experience my share
at the stages for the arts in 2011.

The café is the most integrated place on the planet–Allen Ginsberg

Mole Hole Mode

When I sit at my computer
I'm transported by fantasy
into a universal commuter
awed by ecstasy.

Transported by fantasy
I tunnel in my mole hole
awed by ecstasy
through a cosmic black hole.

I tunnel in my mole hole
to discovery new universes.
Through a cosmic black hole
I seek light for my verses.

To discover new universes
I zone past stars.
I seek light for my verses.
I'm faster than quasars.

I zone past the stars
into a universal commuter.
I'm faster than quasars
when I sit at my computer.

The Clumsy Poet

The syllabic poet stumbles on metric feet.

Rain Signatures

The
rain
scribbles
dribbles down
windows, drops pock
periods on puddle sheets.

Bureaucratic Double Talk

Walled by paper
hanger-ons
execute by delay.

People
penned
away from the novel

trained
to engineer
people in their tracks.

Letters and decisions
comput-erred
to be personal.

Paper backed responses
bound
by hard covered book

sent by unlipped
stamps–
too enveloped to lick

S–L–O–W–L–Y

red tape
worms
through loop holes

Planning Commission Meeting

The mannikin men are called to order.
The gavel's lowered, their lips sealed smiles.
Minutes ready to scratch the surface.
All with a stroke of a ball point pen

click....click

She sits up close to the city's models,
eyes rolling as marbles in play,
lips a scythe, nerves wired,
adjusting hearing aid for static...static

click....click

Her home was yellow, mellowed warm
brushed by trees, paletted by garden
sidewalk cracks tufted green
edges trimmed by clippers

click...click

Then porched, alone, picker not planter–
family albumed, pocketbook pinched,
past tending time, she must sell out.
Sold–in a snap of heels

click...click

"The lot is in a changing neighborhood.
The sidewalk is cracked, the area rundown.
We need more multi-family units.
Re-zone it apartments. All in favor..."

click...click

Ears megaphoning in their ayes,
quivering her needles, supple swords to her bag,
eyes glassing these store window men,
she stumbles to the door.

click...click

City Tree

You grip the earth, alone.
Bark girdled by concrete.
Your seeds hit tombstone.

Seeds are released, then blown
buried by shoveling feet.
You grip the earth, alone.

Barren now. all hope thrown
toward distant dirt retreat.
Your seeds hit tombstone.

Limbs empty, birds have flown,
roots curl in dark defeat.
You grip the earth. Alone.

Branches hover. Below your brown
leaves palm-pat the walk and street.
Your seeds hit tombstone.

Leaves, cradles if seeds are sown,
are caskets. They deplete
you. Grip the earth. Alone,
your seeds hit tombstone.

The Gaping Black Hole

Star orbiting rim of black hole
more hesitant than shot-gun groom of future
gyrating with galactic debris
hissing like an oroborus
pulsating light toward swirling darkness
drawn toward event horizon.

The twinkling star will blink out.

The cosmos controls the stars destiny?
Collisions sent the star on this trajectory?
Any free will among stars?
Our technology can't blast it out of range.
Not guided like our space explorations.
The star is sucked by a cosmic vacuum cleaner,
loses energy to resist. Dark energy? Dark matter?
The star is beyond our ability to release.

The twinkling star will blink out.

A hot, lifeless star might be lead to end its cycle
in the maw of a dark, quenching black hole.
A star at the edge of turbulence,
at the brim of existence splitting its whole
might not have a cosmic chance but to go—
gobbled by a voracious black hole.

The twinkling star will blink out.

Stardust Descendants

When the planet Earth was seeded
with sentient beings. Cosmic
cousins had hopes we would bring light
into the dark, cold universe?

What was the universal plan
when the planet Earth was seeded?
A way-station to other worlds?
Cosmic experiment or pawn?

Or remnants from some distant war?
Or an accidental landing?
When the planet earth was seeded
did they come and leave their DNA?

Earthlings from now alien worlds
rooted and grew new varieties?
Our transplanted roots got shiny
when the planet Earth was seeded?

Word-Playful

Oh, You Beautiful Doll

Act boldly and unseen forces will come to your aid. Dorothea Brande

When I was single doll mother at ten,
some neighbor boys made fun of my baby.
The Raggedy Anne was scruffy, maybe
but my motherly instincts kicked in, then.
I chased the three boys to their homes and when
I caught them beat them up in turn, you see
they insulted baby's inner beauty.
One father laughed as I whooped his abashed son.
My father dragged me home—but I had won.

On Mother's Day

Grandparents return grandson to daughter on Mother's Day.
They load the car with his backpack and electronic gear.
Grandson umbilicals his IPOD to the radio,
negotiates volume and quietly texts on his cell phone.

Grandpa focuses on driving. Backseat, Grandma distracts
herself from loud, offensive, foul-language lyrics,
slam-bam, crap-rap rhythms, demeaning,
degrading use of mother in a hyphenated word.

Head and heart-throbbing Grandma struggles with pounding sounds.
She tries to pick out triple rhymes of hip hop but hears
Baby, baby, baby–I love you! I love you baby, baby baby.
Women are not babies. Her grandson is a teen.
Grandma groans and tries to quell futile, oft-stated criticism.

Finally–Michael Jackson with "Billie Jean", "Man in the Mirror",
"Beat it".
Grandma chimes in and writhes rhythms in her seatbelt.
She sings to join, not blot out the tunes,
but tone-deaf guys plead for her to stop.

Grandson silently texts. Grandma seethes for suffrage.
Painful words and songs continue to trouble her.
He has loving cards and gifts for Grandma and Mom.
Grandma waits for disconnection from discordant notes to deliver her.

Palm Sunday Service in Assisted Living

Visitors and staff with clients
struggling to be self-reliant
docilely sit in lined-up chair.
Soon the young pastor is aware
after Bible verses, hymns, psalms in their behalf
to give palms to the clients, visitors and staff.

Prayers and praise holding fronds tight
some do not get meaning quite right.
Some begin to chew Easter palms.
One woman leaves, having some qualms.
Man shouts "Let's get the hell out of here" to hell-raise?
All exit room in need of some prayers and praise.

Poetry Verses Prose

Poetry is tight–terse, constipated,
not like the diarrhea of prose.

The white on a poetry page lets more light through
than the dark shade blocks of prose.

Poets control the line and design the page.
Prose meanders margin to margin.

The variety of forms keeps poets puzzling
to find the best way to express ideas.
Prose has fewer sparkles, images and metaphor per line.

Prose is a movie reel to tell a story.
Poetry can tell it in one frame.

Prose can be too long and tedious to read.
With a poem the agony stops sooner, but can linger just as long.

Poetry conveys the impact quicker.
Prose delivers more punches before knocking you over.

Crack Up

There is a crack in everything.
That's how the light gets in...Leonard Cohen

I'll try to be a crackerjack of poetry–
a safe cracker to creativity,

crackle the surface with lines of a poem–
let the light pour out and in,

crack down on distractions and avoid crack-ups,
illuminate darkness like a firecracker with a light-hearted crack.

The crack in my voice could crack open enlightenment,
crackdown on my tendency toward judgments. I'll make wise cracks.

Though I may be considered a crackpot or cracked,
that is not what I've cracked up to be.

Without the negative connotations of crack
my cracks could scar the darkness, heal with light.

Chatoyant
Having a changeable luster or color with an undulating band of white light.
Webster's New Collegiate Dictionary

I am loosely attached to this planet,
choose to dwell in the airways of angels
wear a dimmed halo at a tilted angle,
wing it, reluctant to touchdown.
I am an immigrant from the multiverse,
live fourteen simultaneous lives.

I am star-stuff collaged into flesh
journey this incarnation toward light and love.
I am heavy on the Earth, but prefer lighter weight,
escape to ethereal domains in better, vivid dreams
or work out trials in ephemeral contrast realms,
wake relieved for another chance.

I am in essence a dusty, curious, cosmic spirit
who chose this life time to play with words
who selected carefully family and friends
and landscapes with diverse delights
who uses imagination as my guide–
somewhat ambivalent about my assignment.

I am supposed to be a dedicated light-worker,
seek enlightenment for a transformative shift.
I am from star-quarks twinkling my soul
who darkles with darkness
who sparkles with dawn
facing sunset with anticipation.

Omni-Me

Are we sparked quarks of an omni-one?
Do we have doppelgangers galore?
Do we live in more than one dimension?

Do we choose one life to focus on or won?
Do we decide after transition some more?
Are we sparked quarks of an omni-one?

Do we have over-souls over every one
of our multi-dimensional lives we explore?
Do we live in more than one dimension?

Is there free will for every I in each someone?
Are there some lives we wish to ignore?
Are we sparked quarks of an omni-one?

I guess too many is better than being no one.
I'd be multiple parts of oneness at my core.
Do we live in more than one dimension?

All these realities can stun
if we open each cosmic door.
Are we sparked quarks of an omni-one?
Do we live in more than one dimension?

Conceiving Multiples

Poetry is an effort to escape from the material realities to spiritual values.
The Urantia Book

If we believe life threads one needle of Godliness,
one universe—just one all encompassing Prime Source,
the concept of multiverse and multiple dimensions
could embroider belief systems, yank us off course.

If we believe in unfurling curled-up dimensions,
and examining the universes polka-dotted
in dark energy cosmic fabric pattern—
maybe our remnant theory snags can be spotted.

If we believe in a potential heaven
or some form of achievable after-life,
the concept of multiplicate dead-end places
could unravel re-vision, stitch strife.

If we believe we are alone
in this one universe and God chosen,
the concept of other alien-to-us sentient beings
could find this heated debate—unfrozen.

If we believe in one explosive Big Bang
set off by one incomprehensible igniter,
the concept of infinite Big Bangs throughout time
could illuminate our darkled view brighter.

If we believe we are strung along by string theory
and the Big Bang is the whole shebang,
manifold theories to the contrary
may cause our knowledge to boomerang.

If we believe ancient starlight traveling through spacetime
leads to enlightenment of our cosmic past, spark
repulsive gravity, Dark Energy expanding galaxies apart—
it is like finding a quark in the dark.

Why not singularity to multiplicity? Innumerable
cosmic creators whose domains constantly expand?
Our imaginations can follow new trajectories
as our new options and insights command.

Multitudinous theories of physics and math
are not the only paths to knowing.
Add intuition, creativity, breakthrough ideas.
There are myriad ways of mind-blowing

Droning

Drones
fly
to kill,
monitor.
Drones do distant work
unseen and unaccountable.

Male
drones
stingless
honey bees.
Parasite person,
loafer lives off other's labor.

Drone
is
remote
controlled and
radio-controlled.
Computer targets enemies.

Drone
is
dull hum,
same sound thrums.
Not music to ears
who dislike all monotonous.

Veteran's Day 11-11-11

Dangling from dewy, empty mailbox
a snaring spider web etches sky,
semi-camouflaged in fog.

No mail delivery to disturb this web.
The mailbox bordered between
sidewalk and street is shut tight.

In the street grandson and grandpa
wearing woolen caps, toss a hard rubber football,
run on wet asphalt.

On the sidewalk cheerleader grandma
seated in a red camp chair, huddles in a furled
red cape like a bullfighter's before the fight.

Grandson played eighth grade football
but ended that battlefield after one season
to his grandma's great relief.

Grandpa, a soccer player, non-combat
Vietnam War ROTC vet practiced battle yet left
the Army for graduate school before deployment.

Now grandson and grandpa prefer basketball,
play catch with baseballs and footballs
on less violent fields of action.

Grandson throws football to grandma.
Her fingers sting and hurt in the attempt to catch.
Guys went to get a softer ultimate composite football.

At noon all go to women's basketball game.
At night all go to women's volleyball game.
Youthful grandma could not play most sports or go to war.

Veterans on many different fields
play their games by often other's rules.
Grandma prefers non-violent fields and peace marches.

Fragile web clings to catch sustenance.
Gently windblown, web will unravel soon.
Now grasping guardian glistens in autumnal sun.

Sometimes

Sometimes life accumulates like an ironworks slagheap.
Sometimes there are heavy places with sharp edges.
Sometimes there is heat in the process of becoming.
Sometimes life is hard or flows molten.
Sometimes our form is fluid–pours into molds.
Sometimes sparks explode light.
Sometimes there is shine.
Sometimes we temper steel.

Sunflower

Yellow
mellow
bright sunflower
from dark
they spark
centered power.

Thrusting
busting
open to glow
I breed
sun seed
from my window.

Naming Ceremony for the White Bison Calf

A very cool vibe, kind of like a cross between Woodstock and the Nativity–
Bill Varsell

On top of a hill-top in Goshen, Connecticut
overlooking grazing bison on Mohawk Bison Farm
Lakota, Mohawk, Seneca and Cayuga tribal elders
joined hundreds of others to name the rare, pure, white calf
a symbol of hope and unity to Native Americans.
"Called" crowds lining the fence witnessed the private ceremony
despite rain
which Native Americans considered a blessing,
some suffering drought.

Under an arbor amid thunder and lightning, a good omen,
Marian and Chubb White Mouse from the Oglala Lakota tribe
came from South Dakota to lead the naming ceremony.
Marian White Mouse said the birth of the white bison
was a sign from a prophet who helped them endure
famine and strife.
"We come with one prayer and one mind. This is truly a
miracle."
One prayer will keep us together. A hawk circled overhead.

Barbara Threecrow, a Naticoke tribe elder from New York
sat holding a sacred Canupa of beaver skin containing a pipe.
The name came through the spirits. "I believe this is an
awakening. This is a way to tell people to remember the
sacredness of all life."
With songs and drum beats, in traditional garb, they celebrated.
Purified by sage smoke, some loaned umbrellas, no electronics
joyous people named the playful calf, "Yellow Medicine Dancing
Boy."

Naming the "God Particle"

What gives all matter size and shape?
Why does matter have mass,
combine with gravity? Gape.
Scientists went to head of class.
They think they found "God Particle."

Riddle Higgs Boson nicknamed God.
Particles attract, then
mass bigger. Years researchers prod
not knowing theory when
they think they found "God Particle."

Will this help prove Big Bang theory?
Know the subatomic role?
Delivered concept for weary?
Theory now more than a poll?
They think they found "God Particle".

"God Particle" is laymen term.
Higgs Boson footprint found
and a shadow hint smash at CERN.
Not as certain as sound.
They think they found "God Particle."

Free Flying

Multi Verses

I could write multi-verses on multiverses
if I fully grasped the concept.
I can't write a uni-verse
on the universe either.
I do not know how many dimensions
my sentient essence resides concurrently.

Scientists proclaim parallel universes,
eleven dimensions, bubbled galaxies,
string theory, m-theory,
brane bumping brane in flat or curved universes.
In different dimensions we could be living alternative lives.
Perhaps deceased loved ones thrive in another reality
and our dreams are experienced there.
Who knows where our consciousness travels and dwells?
Scientists have not developed their Theory of Everything
for this planet let alone all the possible universes.

Invisible to our limited sensory equipment
all these alternate perceptions of being,
simultaneous lives connected to our individual selves
take deviations from our currently lived trajectory.
In many dimensions I could live variations of choices.
My mistakes in this realm might not be taken in another realm.
My talents and contributions could be greater,
my journeys' impacts more beneficial elsewhere.

How do other beings in other dimensions influence me
here or anywhere my spirit exists?
Perhaps heaven is just one of these dimensions
and as our qi leaves Earth, it has options.
I thought I'd go to the Pleiades next incarnation,
but maybe I should see what other dimensions
and the multiverse might be offering.

If I could recall my many lives in many dimensions,
maybe I could write multi-verses of times in multiverses.
Cosmic couplets, quarky quatrains, celestial syllabics,
galactic ghazals, fusion free verse, numinous nonce forms–
spark light in dark energy,
brain on brane with poetic license
explore the infinite of the cosmos.

The Only Ones

They live wondering if they are the only ones, knowing only the wish to
know and the great black distance they–we–flicker in.
Tracy Smith "My God It's Full of Stars"

In dimensions, on planets, bubbled branes they ask
Where does sentience reside? Does it need bodies?
Particles and sparticles, quarks and sparks glomming
are roaming knowing and unknowing light and dark.
Consciousness is exploring, experiencing
essence with or without visible equipment.
Some light streaks multiverses, warps wormholes, space/time.
Light-lives leap through darkness–spears, shards, glowing embers.
Surrounded by unseen beings I am not alone.
I seek light so I might see in shadowed darkness.
But some beings might not need light to live or know.
The transformations to host life are infinite.

I'm in this body on this planet for this time
but energy quintessence of soul recycles
through time, space, realities ephemeral or
solid with an invisible guiding system.
Along for the ride perhaps with cosmic groupies.
Changing cosmic companions I might not travel
with openly and not always recognize or
consult. Alone, I navigate, try to control
but go with the flow toward love–freely and bravely.
If life has meaning anywhere, who creates it?
We are not the only ones asking this question.
We're not the only ones seeking life in the dark.

Are We Really Alive?

Where does consciousness live?
Does it survive
only where we think it is alive?

Do souls dwell only in flesh
or do they mesh
in other dimensions and refresh?

What does it mean to be living?
What is awareness giving?
What are all the clues sieving?

What do we really know?
As far as senses go
our equipment is only so-so.

Am I really actually here?
All I hold dear
is not what it would appear?

What about the world of dreams–
a reality it seems?
Where are the boundaries or seams?

Alive? It is only a guess.
If I must assess
I can muster an unqualified yes.

Evolving Hominids to Homo Sapiens

Brain's "big bang"
symbols clang
knowledge rang.
Modern gang
E.T. sprang?

DNA
sparks the way
to our day.
Changes stay?
New ones stray?

Across void
asteroid
with life buoyed.
Can't avoid
sequence toyed?

Early man
and woman
also-ran
find they can
get human.

Multidimensional Being

Some folks predict Earthlings are about to shift
from 3-D to the 4th or 5th dimension.
They say newcomers are being born
with enhanced DNA to adjust to this shift.

Already I believe in reincarnation
and not the one-shot-is all deal.
Maybe in a past life I paid indulgences
for after-life or next-life insurance.

I am pondering being multidimensional
living simultaneous lives in several dimensions.
Some folks say we average about three lives
in this universe. Talk about love triangles.

It's similar to the aboriginal Dream Time
when this lifetime is the dream
while living elsewhere, except
if multidimensional this means several realities.

Perhaps when I am dreaming
I am touching base
with my other splinter-selves or soul-slivers
in their home situations.

My dreams surely have introduced
some surreal beings and places.
Perhaps when I'm weary of this focused life
I sleep and travel to concurrent lives.

Conditions could be better or worse elsewhere.
When I use up this weighty 3-D body
and take my qi to another container or frequency
I wonder where my next sentient location will be?

Maybe this upcoming shift to 4th or 5th dimension
which I may or may not be ready for
could open a new enlightening path
and delay another transfer for awhile.

Perhaps this multidimensional juggling
gives me chances or choices to lighten
the cosmic darkness where light beings
are more luminous than the stars.

Congress of My Splintered Soul

As I approach the end of this earthly life,
I would like to make an informed decision
on what my next life style incarnation might be
and if I have any choice in the options.
So I send this cosmic petition
into the multiverse for information.

Do I have to die before I have access
to the Akashic records or
learn sequential sentience procedures?
Can I receive enlightenment in the dream or meditative state,
out-of-body journeying, frequency or dimensional shifts
that will guide me to further cosmic experiences?

How do I deliver this request? To some Cosmic Network?
Through prayer, meditation, consciousness experiments,
channeling, medium, psychic, conscious dreaming,
chanting, a ritual procedure, mind-altering substances?
Would a megaphoned, sonic yelp get attention?

But who would I get? A cosmic clerk on Life Style Requests,
guardian angels, spirit guides,
dimensional directors
reincarnational soul selectors?

To start, I would like to request a conference
of my simultaneous, multi-dimensional selves
to plan the trajectory of my soul.
I would like some time to re-unite and contemplate
what I am learning from my multiple lives--
then explore past and simultaneous multi-mes
or I Ams from basic oneness.

Can I open the Akashic records of my past lives
and perhaps peek at future destinations?
Can we warp space/time? Is communication possible?
Can I re-unite my simultaneous lives

in many dimensions and locations in one spot
or tele-conference? Very distance viewing?
A cosmic communion could gather my multi-faceted sentience
into an Oversoul mosaic, soul- splinters like stitches
to create life art instead of confused chaos.

I could encounter static, glitches, frequency jamming,
bureaucracy with a cosmic clerk stating:
Before your request is under review
by the Soul Oversight and Arbitration Board,
you must go through proper channels
and follow protocol and procedures.
Your guides must confer to see
if your request is warranted
and in your soul's best advancement.
The multiversal plan has certain parameters.
There are forms to fill out for several steps.
You must get cooperation
from all your current operating selves
to intrude into their sovereignty.

Let's see. You have 14 currently conscious
operating systems in several dimensions.
Each dimension has its own rules.
Free will is not universal.
Some selves might prefer to remain inviolate
and/or are not interested, unavailable..
You might have communication barriers
due to varying frequencies and symbolic codes.
Of course there is culture shock.
You have many manifestations
and your Earthling equipment–
well, might require some adjusting. Technical assistance.

There is a need for interpreters,
mediators, guidance counselors, spacial relations
to work on goals on multiple life charts.
The arbitration board would need good evidence
as to why you feel this soul search is necessary

and why you are so impatient to just let your process evolve.
A rammy Aries on Earth could have universal implications.
Why can't you go with the flow
and not disrupt so many entities?

You would need to do research into past lives
to see where the seeds for your needs arise.
What unfinished business needs completing in this Earth life?
What do you hope to understand by getting **you** all together?

You need a plan with topics to discuss with the participants.
What do you hope to achieve from this congress
of mini-bits, splinters of your cosmic being?
Where and how do you hope to meet?
In bodies, thought forms, holograms?
Reduce to thought level and leave life vehicles behind?
Who would operate these systems left unattended?
Walk-ins? Shards of your soul operating
at minimal, coma-level capacity? How long would you be gone?
Would you be allowed to return to full-functioning
if you had dysfunctional out-of-bodies experiences?
Perhaps you could consider video conferencing
by cosmic electronic means like your Skype.
The logistics could be staggering.

Obviously you have not thought
of all the ramifications of your request.
Do you really want to intrude into your other life charts?
The other life styles and relationships you have forged
in many configurations, which if they transform to meet
in a common place with a common form and frequency
could jeopardize your returning transmutations
to fulfill your other roles.
What if some decide to bale or become voyeurs
on your more dynamic, creative soul sparticles?
You could unbalance your essence evolution
which you are gaining from diverse experiences.

Trying to unify your soul's purpose
seems limiting not enhancing.
Try to accept a cosmic plan is in place .
Perhaps you are not to know
your full expansion possibilities or your Oversoul
which has its own perspective on your multi-selves.

By the way, you would need your Oversoul's permission
to inquire into your soul's secrets.
Your Oversoul would have to grant access
to all your life expressions should the board
deliberate in your favor.

You have reached a possible intermediary
for your earthly aspect to your multi-dimensional wholeness.
All work in behalf of your oneness, your Oversoul.
Who are you to question and tamper with your cosmic plan?

O.K. Put me through to my Oversoul
or better yet–the Prime Creator.
This splinter of multiple-me has issues.

Cosmic Concepts

If the Creator is curious
and seeds specks of sentience
in beyond-counting beings
all over the cosmos
what is the purpose?
How does this omnipotent essence
follow the unfoldings
of these creations?

If the Creator is benevolent
why create evil at all?
Why balance positive and negative energy?
Why not all live together
in harmony and not have
all the hassle of trying to create it?

If the Creator wants the only
constant to be change,
why all the painful experiments?
Can't chaos be observed away
from beings that prefer
love over fear
nurturing over pain?

If the Creator decreed
a free will planet for earth
why all the alleged alien DNA
tampering and interventions?
The anticipated dimension shifts?
Why does force have to be a choice
when it prevents the free will of others?

If the Creator is a spectator
and inventor of all the forms there are,
why all the violent trauma?

If the Creator could free creative lives
for the benefit of all beings,
then I could believe the universe is kind.

Perhaps the Creator is not infallible
and learning on the job? Or retired?
What if the Creator is a committee?
Now that does not evoke
cosmic confidence.

Surfing the Waves of the Cosmos

Rippling through the cosmos—
sound waves, light waves, gravitational waves,
elements, energy,
black holes, white holes, worm holes,
splatter of matter,
sparks of quarks,
radiation, particle zoo
dark energy and dark matter
into the Dark Flow
from nothing, no when, no where
or parallel world collisions?
Big Bang beginning from an initial singularity?
Two flat parallel brane worlds colliding?
New theories churn cosmological tsunamis.

Our particular universe may have begun
from an infinitely small singularity
about 13.7 billion years ago—
an unbelievably hot blast
which inflates incredibly fast
cools to create our universe
toward a Big Crunch or Big Chill
to deflate and start all over—
a bombastic balloon?

Or was it like two flat sheets of bubble wrap
and we are one universe bubble within the sheet.
These brane worlds collide
and inject each other with energy
spreading out for brilliant eons
then undulate into other cycles of collisions.
A fourth dimension sandwiched
between two 3-D worlds?
Bouncing branes collide and separate
splitting open and closing the sandwich?
What holds the sandwich? How many sandwiches?
When is our particular bubble ready to pop?
What bursts our bubble?

Is the fabric of space/time wrinkled or ironed out?
Have we seen the edge of our visible universe?
All the hidden dimensions and brane boundaries
can be wiggling, elastic and very close?
M-Theory says there are eleven dimensional
space and parallel universes–
ten of space and one of time?
String Theory is entangled and strangled.
There are waves spiraling outward from Earth–
one wave creates another and as it circulates it grows
and refines to become pure sound and pure wave.
How can we comprehend these invisible worlds?

Supposedly Dark Energy expands to cool
the heated ignition of everything.
Currently a certain uniformity exists
as earth sprawls
from our perceive shifting neighbors.
Continuous cycles recycle ingredients
into infinite multiverses and configurations.
We do not know what came before this endless process.

Whether like a clang of cymbals–the Big Clang
Or the blast of a cherry bomb–The Big Bang
or some other cycle or beginning,
how were the ingredients formed
and what Creator glommed them
into becoming
and ignited existence?
When did sentience enter the mix
so we knew something happened?

Surfing the currents of cosmic waves
adrift but afloat,
bobbling with theories
on the throbbing megabites
of a silent cosmos,
I await elucidation
from a more enlightened essence
perhaps Garrett Lisi
as he surfs waves to perfect
An Exceptionally Simple Theory of Everything.

Not Knowing

When they try to explain
the vastness of the universe,
my lack of affinity to numbers
is not relevant.
Even if I grasped infinity
and this universe
there are multiverses
and multiple dimensions
to contend with.

My affection for letters
doesn't help either
in trying to connect words
to comprehend
the unknowable,
the incomprehensible.

Without symbols to process
the seeable and unseen
my brain just blanks out.
Sentience just goes so far.
I definitely will never be
a know it all.

Celestial Clean-up
For space mess, scientists seek celestial broom... Kenneth Chang

Chicken Little, the sky is falling!
Space junk is falling in chunks and pieces
an overcrowded traffic jam.
Many nations own the celestial debris.
Many nations must clean up after themselves.

A defunct NASA satellite crashed in a jam.
Failed Russian probe in smithereens, left debris.
The International Space Station dodges pieces.
20,000 pieces of space junk collide with themselves.
Bring out nets, drag them to Earth to prevent falling!

If they collide they can create more pieces.
But nations don't want to monitor themselves.
Junk shatters in 17,000 miles per hour crashes leaving debris.
Satellite operators can dodge big stuff, but little junk's falling
leaving Earth's near neighborhood in a jam.

GPS, weather warnings, hurricanes threatened by debris.
Space junk can be tethered to prevent falling.
But nations still working on codes of conduct for themselves.
Meanwhile space junk and communications continue in a jam.
Just who is going to pick up the pieces?

Nations must stop space pollution themselves.
Chicken Little Syndrome leaves us in a jam.
We join in shouting: Chicken Little the sky is falling!
The US Air Force tracks 20,000 orbiting space junk pieces.
The Kessler Syndrome deals with problem of space junk debris.

Falling space junk pieces jam communication devices
and cause debris by colliding with themselves.

All About Nothing

Scientists are studying nothing.
To think of nothing is something.
We know almost nothing about Dark Matter.
Of Dark Energy we know but a smatter.

To think of nothing is something.
So does knowing nothing matter?
Of Dark Energy we know but a smatter.
Space can't be made of vast nothing.

So does knowing nothing matter?
Just because we can't see it doesn't make it nothing.
Space can't be made of vast nothing.
Did the Big Bang make something scatter?

Just because we can't see it doesn't make it nothing.
We know almost nothing about Dark Matter.
Did the Big Bang make something scatter?
Scientists are studying nothing.

The World Has Too Much

The world has too much with us,
veiled in pollution, melting away.
The world is tired of global fuss
and is likely to change our wasteful way.

The world might find a way to die
and end our days in this dimension.
We are too abundant. We could try
to elevate deeds toward retention.

The world might weed people from this garden
and living things might pass away too.
People could ask for universal pardon
before someone releases a new particle zoo.

Fouling the planet has consequences.
Can we ameliorate the dire sequences?

Dust to Dust

Drifting inside
the living room
in slants of skylight,
my dust vacations
from intermittent,
infrequent dust rags
and capped dust sprays.
Stirred to travel
by will-o-wisps
and resettling after
a twisting tryst in air,
from heat bursts,
door slams,
window venting–
dust returns to new digs.
Textile fiber, sprigs of insulation,
dander, pollen,
ordinary orts,
dander, pollen,
bug bits, mites and tics
await to surface,
join the rest home
to cloud the shine
to patina metals and woods.

My motes in motion
appear in another light
when I know
they have me covered.
I can neglect dusting
for another day
imagining stardust
joining in the whirl.

Dental Appliance

The new refrigerator
juts from the counter gum line
like a buck tooth.
Flawlessly white
it roots on the cork floor.
We load the fridge
with some diet and organic foods;
place magnets,
spots of decay;
admire the sleek smile-curved handles.
We are satisfied
it is a simple model
without the braces of decadent technology,
no ice and water dispensers.
Just green water bottles
grinning on the inside door.

Chilling Drive to Crater Lake in June

On her 17th birthday, third week on permit
after off-key chorus of happy birthday, she drives.
Dad is "smart media" assistant and coach.
Grandparents backseat map-readers and critics.

Her arctic air-conditioning flares sun-reddened hair.
Passengers don coats and chatter.
Her aunt texts LOL which Grandma thinks
means lots of luck.

She negotiates mountainous curves and freeway,
road construction monitored by flaggers and lights,
swims with road-whales and curses
tail-gaters and passers swishing on scenic by-ways.

Music helps her focus. Driving suggestions annoy.
At the park entrance the I-Phone play-list blares
girl girl girl girl yeah yeah yeah yeah–yeah yeah yeah yeah girl girl girl girl
At caldera's viewpoints she holds "meetings" on her cell.
Stops hold photo ops for her family's "volcanic legacy."

East-side snowbound. West-side snow-banks higher than the car.
Contrail scars blue sky reflected in pure blue lake.
Snow-capped mountains feather the water's rim–
the deepest U.S. lake with remnant Wizard Island.

A place of power. A place of tribal rituals and vision quests.
A place for midge flies to lay eggs on the water's surface.
Eggs drop nearly 2000 feet, larvas feed on bottom bio-matts,
mature to pupae, wriggle and float to the surface as adults and fly.

She has warmed and reduced air-conditioning.
Returning home she commands silence, chills
directional disagreements. "Dad, you always have to look for me
and I can do it myself" She drives unfamiliar back roads home.

GPS glitch loops them through Glide and Colliding Rivers.
Back on track, discussions resume. Justin Bieber booms
Girl, I'm in love with the thought of. I'm in love with the thought of you, girl.
Grandma thinks he sings: Girl I'm in love with your daughter.
Dad creates a cell video of the debate en route.

A flagger with a stuffed monkey clutching the stop sign
wishes her agnates Happy Fathers Day weekend
before the pilot car guides her across a bridge.
She wonders why flagger did not greet female side of the car.

The family celebrates at supper at Steamboat Springs
then a traditional ice cream shop at Rice Hill. Quietly
they ride, drinking Smart Water in warm setting sun.
Tomorrow she will drive her Dad to the airport.

She will board a plane for California
to visit her mother with a shift car to practice.
In a few months she'll leave for college.
Like the midge fly, she's driven to flight.

Declarations of Independence

Your closet gapes empty.
Walls stare bare.
Nothing of you remains in the room
but memories.
Your life left in boxes.
Your furniture taken.
A new rug covers your floor scars.
Paint will whitewash walls
stripped of Lamborghini and macho men posters
now rolled
and rock stars now in scrapbooks.
Only nails like thorny reminders
to tug from dirty, white walls.

But wait– on your closet shelf
was a lair of stuffed animals–
a soft and cuddly remnant
from the zoo of childhood.
I open the door.
They're gone.
I close the hollow door and survey
flatness, the colorless room.
Only the curtains wink open and close
to encourage your and my independence.

Outside a Window

Outside my childhood bedroom window
in the hot dark
beyond the squared wooden panes
rimmed with crackled white paint
my dead father stands
beside the backyard lamp post
waiting for me to notice him
as my intuitive friend has.

He watches me clear out his home
he shared with my mother
for almost fifty years.
His father built this Cape Cod home
for my parent's wedding present
during the Depression to keep
skilled Swedish construction workers employed.
My father guards memories within each packed
and hauled- away box with treasured items.

I sense his presence
as my possessions reveal themselves
from soft-lined drawers, jammed closets
and from metal under bed storage.
I must decide the fate of my childhood student papers,
junk jewelry, paper dolls in envelopes, photos,
my mother's clothes, the furniture.
I must make a choice of what to save and give away.

Standing at the window looking
at the automatically lighted lamp post
my father installed,
I can't see the phantom of my father
who, when I was a child in this room,
urged me from this window
to climb back from the adjacent garage roof
as I gazed at stars.

For over twenty years after his death,
my mother, now in a nursing home, slept in this room.
The night stars, dimmed by pollution
are faint specks of light.
My friend said my father wore a blue suit
like in my mother's vision she saw at the end of her bed
where her husband stood with her father and grandson.

How I wish I could see my grandfather, father and son
gathered around that lamp post
saying farewell to this house
waving to me at this window.

Disconnected

Someone is missing.
     Someone is a missing link
     from a chain of possible events.
        A woman I think.

She is not on Facebook Twitter A Google map
     She has no GPS   No cell phone
        No land line to trace residence.
     She probably lives alone.

She might have dropped out of school
     leaving no forwarding address.
She may have lived out of state
     leaving her home life a mess.

She has no debit or credit cards.
     No IPhone IPod   IPad
        Her "I" is missing.
She reveals no Mom or Dad.

No government check. A false name?
Social security card a fraud?
     Has she accomplished anything
     anyone would applaud?

She's not in an institution   Or in a hospital
Too sane to be caged.   Too young for Medicare.
If we were to look for her
     She could be almost anywhere.

No paper trail to guide us. No pieced puzzles
     to her authentic self.
No electronic detectors   No Internet
     No computer on her shelf

We don't know her livelihood
        Does she still exist?
Is she paid under the table
        living by hand or fist?

She could conceal by identity theft
        might not register to vote   Or drive
                join no organizations   Hold no memberships
She has her own rules to survive.

No numbers follow her   No record of prescriptions
No resumes   Applications   No evidence of addictions
No incarcerations   No expressed convictions
No mug shots   Blogs   Web-sites   No visual depictions

No MRI   No mammogram   No Cat-Scan   No x-ray
Nothing to invade inside
        We do not know if she is   O.k.
Her blood remains   Undrawn.

What does she think?   Or feel?
        Street smart?   In the know?
Does she check lost and found?
        Stash her cash   Or let it flow?

To be unknown is preposterous–
the stereotypical "she" anonymous.
        Shielded by burka   Or wrapped in a shroud
        an alien stranger   In a crowd

Perhaps she is a Luddite
        or captive in a cult
Perhaps she makes her own choices
        whether or not an adult.

No video   No DVD   No photographs
No celebrations   No testimonies
No test results   No tapes or polygraphs
No certificate   Or ceremonies

No donations   No receipts   No documents
No legal birth certificate   No passport
     Nothing that truly identifies   A faceless Amish doll
erased pencil lead   smudged ink   Nothing to report.

What is her occupation
     What prompts her participation
          Does she have a preoccupation
               Passion   Or dream vocation?

She has no "real" numbers.   No label.
     No voice in public affairs
Left or right leaning?   Balanced in the center?
Experienced racial or gender discrimination? Does she care?

She espouses no known causes
     who   or what   she loves   unknown
She is a silhouette   or shadow   in a fogbow.
     We do not know if she's alone.

Does she seek peace and love? Find companionship within?
Does her auric signature resonate?
Is her carbon footprint–light?
Does she walk harmoniously   Or aimlessly journey
with darkened spirit?
Is she yearning for discovery?   Is she powerless with fright?

No DNA chemical blueprint   Or external fingerprint
     Has she denied our oneness?
She shows no appearance in herstory
     They anticipate she wants to be in hiding.
Is the necklace broken?
     They suspect she might be me.

How Many Children Do You Have?

At a fund-raising party for charity,
a stranger asks, "How many children do you have?"
To me it is not a topic for idle cocktail chatter
but a sobering issue.
So it depends–two or three.
Is it a healthy dark chocolate or sweetened milk chocolate day.

It depends who asks.
Two for doctors who have medical reasons
to know my live births.
Three to the counselor if dealing with grief.
The number depends on the degree of acquaintance
and necessity.
I birthed two sons and we berthed an adopted daughter.

It depends on the context.
Does the inquisitor want to know how many naturally born–two,
number chosen–one. All three were wanted and beloved.
One son died in 1982.
Do they want to know how many children are alive or dead?

I ask myself how much do they really want to know.
If I say once three and now just two
will they really want to know how one son died
or would it be too much information?
Do they need more than the number?
Names, ages, gender, where they are now?
Even grandchildren are beyond baby pictures sharing stage.

Is the question a sneaky way to ask how
I got so much gray hair?
Do I have step-children
and how many fathers and mothers are involved?
Two mothers, one alive –me and one dead before we found her.
Two fathers, one my husband and one unidentified.

How much do I want to reveal?
How healed am I at the moment?
Those who know me well, know the answers
and know how to ask questions
about my children carefully and openly.
Fluid dark chocolate sauce or hardened Milk Duds today?

On this occasion I gave a charitable dark M and M response,
say "three". I remember some people can't conceive children
and ask a different question.

The Angel Collector

In dreams to other worldly places,
unfamiliar glowing shops
in celestial settings
beckon me to select
miniature angels for my collection.
In narrow diffusely-lit alleys, bright blockish malls
or inside an alien metallic shiny sphere–
hand-sized angels await my inspection,
displayed on well-lit shelves, in baskets,
or clustered brilliantly on artificial trees.
The angels exude internal light- incandescent
enlighten my path angel to angel.
In my palm I study each unique,
delicate, numinous angel
ecstatically finding several
to bring home with me.

But when I awake empty-handed,
I do not see any of my earthly interpretations
as exquisitely expressed as those gossamer replicas
closer to the ethereal, eternal angelic spirits.
However, in my earthly-created collection
sprawling on quilted clouds, on hooks,
attached by tacks to walls, tied to hangers,
huddled on chairs, sentinels on shelves and counters–
the angels I can hold in my eyes and hands
still touch my heart with their diversity:
wings of wire, twigs, fabrics, shell, pewter, tin;
halos entwined like nests, smooth rings of metal, plastic,
ribbon, cord; gowns from cotton, ceramic, cookie dough,
horsehair, wood, felt, lace, pop cans, porcelain, paper, pine cone.
Thousands of combinations of texture and color entrance me,
excite my imagination, lead me to conduct
the Hallelujah Chorus in their silent midst.

None of these earth-bound angels have the surreal
luminescence of the dream angels.
Solidly grounded in this reality, lovingly-rendered,
my quirky, humanly-imaged angels
remind me of my elusive dream angels–
the non-collectible, irreproducible, intangible ones
illuminating another dimension.

Dream angels propel me to believe
in other realms, an astral plane,
an afterlife on the Other Side–
places where other essences
love collecting angels
just like I do.

Honey Angel

Pigeon-toed, hands crossed on chest,
the wire-twirled hair, beige gowned
mouthless, small ceramic angel
peered at me from the glass shelf
in the coastal gift gallery.
She reminded me of Raggedy Anne,
beloved by my mother
whom everyone called Honey.

I picked up this barefoot angel,
inspected her brown wings
with a golden star in the center,
followed the stitches outlining
the wings and hem.
Stuck to her feet was a white tag:
Honey
$11.95.

Honey sending me a birthday gift
from beyond.
Of course I bought the angel,
watched the clerk wrap her
like a mummy,
shrouded in a cloud. I took her home.
Unwrapped from her white, soft cushioned,
stripped of bandage price tag,
I read the messages on her feet.
Love you
Honey and me.

Greeting the Elders

On the day before Mother's Day
two well-scrubbed and pressed
missionary elders of the Church
of Latter Day Saints greeted me
in my black night shirt
with lavender feminist logo,
stocking feet and sleep-swept hair.

I was heading to water my boxed plants
near the front door after a long phone call
concerning my brother's breast cancer.
Their plastic black and white badges
identified them as elders–very young elders.
I complimented them on their spiffy ties
and they complimented me on my angel collection
they could see in the entry and adjoining room.

They assumed the angels meant a Christian background.
I replied background yes, present no.
I invited them to see the angels sprawled on walls,
lolling on shelves and flowing on flat surfaces.
One crewcut elder took a photo.

They also assumed I was a writer
from the free poems box in the front yard.
I told them the angels were not just Christian angels
but creative muses for the writers who write here.

As they left they offered spiritual counsel
for their elder. I assured them I knew
where to turn in a spiritual crisis.
My mother would invite young missionaries for a meal.
She thought their mothers would want someone to feed them.
Then she would pit her faith against theirs and not give an inch.

After these elders left with images of angels,
I thought my mother would have wanted me
to invite them for lunch and debate them.
I chose to nourish them with angels,
shook their hands politely,
smiled at my angels,
left to get dressed in purple sweats
to write.

Ah to be a Nudist

How wonderful to be a nudist.
No concern for fashion design,
strategic tattoos in full display
wondering whose taste is crudest.

For the most polite and the rudest
all-over tans without a line,
no laces to trip on when you play
no taking off clothes for a tryst.

Imperfections hidden in a mist.
When you are cold seek warmer clime.
Scars, scabs, lymphomas in full array,
they're bas relief for those sun-kissed.

Pockets, purses, cards, keys, won't be missed.
Must tone up droopy parts, align
my values and possessions in way
I protect rough spots and feel blissed.

Full Moon of February

Storm moon, moon of snow,
pale white moon of ice
like a beacon you glow.

Budding moon from waxing slice
pocked and bony moon
pale white moon of ice.

Little famine moon seeks a spoon.
Hungry moon like a plate
pocked and bony moon.

Moon when wolves congregate
Moon of when raccoons and baby bears are born,
hungry moon like a plate.

Moon of chilling lovelorn
you're too distant to eavesdrop.
Moon of when raccoons and baby bears are born.

Moon when the trees pop
you're too distant to eavesdrop
storm moon, moon of snow
like a beacon you glow.

Only a Part But a Part with a Purpose
Graffiti by a Covered Bridge

A white realtor's box
laced and staked on wooden pole
blatant against lawn
held firmly by rock wall
holds sheets of poetry.
On the clear, plastic front
are stuck-on, multi-colored letters
proclaiming, "Free Poems. Take one."

At a distance I watch walkers pause,
sometimes paw my poems,
clench the poem in wind,
squint in sun at the whiteness
glare at the fonts,
The helpless poems fall limp
or get stuffed in purses,
jammed in backpacks.

Most viewers look puzzled
and walk away.
Several people told me
they thought the house was for sale,
picked up the poems hastily
without reading the raised letters
encouraging engagement with poetry.

My husband took the box down
when he mowed the lawn,
placed it on the garbage can.
I gasped. How could he trash poetry!
I clasped the box tightly
grabbed the pole quickly
to stab the yard with poems.

Birdsong for the Cherry Pickers

Come chomp cherries on elderly Smith's trees.
Top of the line organically grown cherries.
With a light show of dangling CDs!
Land on a limb with the succulent berries.
       Summer brings sun-filled delights.
       Come and nourish your long flights.

Top of the line organically grown cherries!
Tank up with these tummy pleasers.
No one to stop these take-to-nest carries.
They can't be saved by old geezers.
       And they don't even have a cat!
       Can you imagine old fools like that?

With a light show of dangling CDs
they flash a signal around the yard.
Come and eat all you please.
Life is squishy. Don't look so hard.
       Come and snack. Take a rest.
       Peck and peck. Nestle in a nest.

Land on a limb with these succulent berries,
secure that no one will interfere.
Feast with a troop of friendly fairies.
No one will harm you here.
       Sing your song to the sky.
       Join fairy formations when you fly.

Summer brings sun-filled delights.
Don't fly by this abundant tree.
It's passion for cherries that unites
all winged ones—bird or fairy.
       Ah that luscious scrumptious fruit!
       Toast with birdsong, fiddle, flute!

Come and nourish your long flights
with Smith couple's generous harvest.
We can gorge our appetites.
You are certainly a welcome guest.
>As the cherries color and size-up,
>hope the clueless Smiths don't wise up.

Dance of Sparticles

When my caged quarks are released
from this life's particle zoo
will they dance in cosmic freedom
to glom elsewhere in other realms?

How will my essence re-combine
from sparticles and other mini-bits
to solidify or hologram
for another universal experience?

Will they dance in a form
that eventually attracts partners?
All the energetic transformations
possible to express life—bedazzle.

How many rebirths and reconfigurations
exist for exploration?
I tiptoe, trudge and dance through this experience.

Angels

Angels Can Fly Because They Take Themselves Lightly
Scottish Proverb

In the fourth world
women will grow wings.
Men can be caged by ribs
unless they want to take their own ribs
to sculpt their own wings.
Both can wing it.

I intend to fly.
My scapulas will stretch,
feather strong and soft for flight.
Everything elongates–
bleaching-to-blonde again hair bonfires.
Belly ballast flows into long, lithe legs,
arms grow strong enough to hug
an Old Growth redwood.
Breasts barely bump my culottes.
I'm a lean, green flying machine.

With thousands of angels
from my heavenly collection,
we will check out the planet,
sing the Hallelujah Chorus
or jivey hymns, maybe a rap or two
on a tranquil eardrum.

With balloons for lift
and pinwheel wands in hands
we touch others.
Perk up ears. Strum whiskers.
Tweak tails. Tickle feet.

When we return home–
in the paradise-of-the-week,
we flick off stardust,
inspect dented halos, magically
mend gossamer garb,
and soft scrub pollution from our wings.

We check for any missing feather
fallen near benched Forrest Gumps
or borrowed by birds snitching
to cushion their nests.
Feathers re-fluff if we had a bad-wing day
with a ruffle of the wind.

We squadron with eagles.
Unseen. We are the wings beneath
their weary wings.
We soar with sun-spotted seagulls
over frothy seas which curl
on the shore like wingtips.
We giggle with gaggles of geese
swap puns with swans in ponds.

We strip facades, animate toys,
open petals like winglets to the sky.
Breeze by trees until leaves
flutter like feathers from their limbs.

Over necklaces of highways
beaded by cars,
over colorful gift-boxy houses
tied with driveways or fences,
we peek at people hidden inside
and the presences within.

We tickle joy with unbidden wings.
We lift a heavy prayer.
Still second-string angels
we help the eternal angels
who found Third World Earth Earthlings
hopelessly dense and dark.
They took their light
elsewhere in the universe on vacation,
Sirius, the current Mecca,
to sit it out until there is Peace on Earth
and Earth lightens up a bit.

That leaves us as the beings of light
lifting the Earth on our shoulders.
My wings heighten my awareness
of low life
yet carry me lightly
over burst bubbles,
heavy weights
and downers.

I like the idea of ribbing men.
I like the idea of elevating women.
Women are earth angels
waiting in the wings.

Naming Guardian Angels

My friend's guardian angel's name is James.
My grandson James said mine is named Bill.
I thought my guardian angel's name was David.
But I am not sure of my angel's name still.

My grandson James said mine is named Bill.
I asked him what made him say that name.
He said it just came to him to say Bill.
I named my brother William–the same.

I thought my guardian angel's name was David
because at five I decided to be a boy.
cut my long locks to do what my brothers could,
announced my name David and beamed with joy.

But I am not sure of my angel's name still,
although Bill is a perfectly good selection.
I need to hear the name directly somehow–
the perfect way for detection.

A Musing Angel

Angel, get off my shoulder
and let me drift to sleep.
You're making me smolder
and probing my mind too deep.

Angel, just shoo away.
You've captured my hand.
Gee, it's been a long day.
But now I understand.

You want me to praise you
with an acrostic alphabet.
Angels need attention too.
But I am not ready yet.

My hubby is sleeping
just snoring like a snark.
Night time is keeping
me from writing in the dark.

But my hand grabs a pen
from my black night stand.
Paper gets marked then
by my automatic hand.

But I can't read my writing
by the light of the clock.
I'll get up where there's lighting
and my muse can unlock.

The house is cold, my feet bare
I roam in search of light.
A dictionary opens unaware
it makes my poem more bright.

Feverishly my muse warms me
as words spill on the page.
Nothing touches or harms me
as angels fill my stage.

I am writing for angels.
I am filled with bliss.
Trying all new angles
to merit a muse-kiss.

Muse-Angel Tug-of-Words

Angels, please be with me today
while I'm at work, while I word-play.
Pen on paper, my thoughts withhold.
Muse is on strike. Celestial
guardian, poetry angel
please make balking words manifold.

Ideas unfold when doubt leaves.
Winged words take flight when paper sheaves
see ink-prints of letter imprints.
Your wing-tips touch my muddled mind
clear words for landing, left behind
luminous–fulfilling your stint.

My muse now sprints as angels flee
returning to me with new hints.

Angelic Possibilities

Are
angels
near me–just
out of sight, sound?
Are they really
with me as some have hyped, believed
or just darkled dream?

But
angel
belief comes
with sentience–
hope for light, love
like rainbows after our harder storms.
Angels are fogbows.

Are
angels
cosmic kin?
Universal?
I think we are
multi-dimensional beings–
stardust like angels.

Cosmic Question

Come
close
angel.
I need you.
Speak up. Don't whisper.
I appear deaf to your counsel.
What
can
I do
to relieve
suffering and the
struggling I witness every day?
At
times
in dreams
I glimpse lives
in strange dimensions
and wonder should I go there instead?
What
keeps
me here?
Boundaries
of space, time, choice or
to create connections of love?
We
live
many
lives to learn.
How many more lives must
I survive here until I'm freed?
I
dream
there are
places of
enlightenment and
peace. Where is this possible? Yet?

My Fall From Grace in Newark Airport at Dawn

Before trip, psychic said my chest looked dark
but I would be all right on Eastern flight.
She did not say I would fall in Newark
on my back down the up escalator, might
crunch my abs like shell to make back arc,
bang my head once, then scratched in morning light.
Out of nowhere a man lifts me to top–
an angel who arrived for rescue stop.

Handkerchief to stop head blood, then before
he left he called for help. He disappeared. On shirt
my blood. Off to hospital stunned and sore.
No chest x-ray I knew I was not hurt.
Eleven blue stitches. Escalator
stripes on body. I am hyper-alert.
Unknown angel I never saw helped me
rise up gracefully and heal gratefully.

Pondering Who to Pray To

```
         I    I
      land    am
    to pray   not sure
   to angels  who hears them
winging my prayers  or who receives prayers
for love and light to beloveds  I flap my word wings anyway
```

Honest to God Angels

Concept of angels is inscrutable–
at least it is to me.
Their existence irrefutable
imaginatively.
Angels' demeanor is so appealing
it's too bad they are not more revealing.

They live in a heavenly dimension
without poverty, fear.
The angels are a hopeful suspension
of what we all hold dear.
Angels live in a realm of joy and light
at least if I have the promotion right.

With free will I can believe they are real.
These messengers of love
can uplift what we do, perceive and feel.
But must they stay above?
I'd like to see them down to earth bringing
universal good and creative winging.

Magnificent Avatars

Angels flit from star to star
across multi-verses to star
in galactic dramas near and far.

It does not matter what form you are
they can transform you–you are
your essence–magnificent avatar.

Light and love flows from afar.
Angels shine brightly from afar
in galactic dramas near and far.

Angels prod dream quest ajar,
open and leave your divinity ajar
your essence–a magnificent avatar.

In galactic dramas near and far
your essence–a magnificent avatar.

Perhaps Angels...

Perhaps angels are astral beings
finer than etheric
capable of celestial seeings
their prescriptions generic.

Perhaps angels are capricious leavers.
Their clients of choice
tend to be light-bearing believers
causing them to rejoice.

Perhaps angels are musical.
They can pull strings.
Also very muse-ful
for lyrical word-springs.

Perhaps angels are nosy.
They peer at you
and make things rosy
if they want to.

Perhaps angels are prophetic
proclaimers of your destiny.
What if you are apathetic
or excessively whiney?

Perhaps angels aren't patient
if you are too much of a pill
and not too compliant.
Do they give you free will?

Perhaps angels require imagination.
You have to hope they exist
in some magical configuration–
a dream hard to resist.

What If Angels...

What if angels wore rainbow gowns,
tinted their wing feathers
and wore halos around their necks?

What if angels play more instruments
than horns or strings
and sing all kinds of celestial music
to entertain themselves and unknown beings?

What if angels became earthbound
more visible and helped people
to become their better selves?

What if angels telepathically prompt us
to our best actions
and warn us of impending harm?

What if angels came when requested
and were able to respond
to our urgent pleas?

What if our stereotypes of angels
are true and we have not imagined
the full extent of their magnificence?

What if our misconceptions about angels
clutter our comprehension
of cosmic consciousness
and angelic realms are not accessible?

What if angels are creative manifestations
to help us cope and inspire
our attempts of love and service?

What kind of angelic attunement
do Earthlings need to know
what is cosmically possible?

What if the angelic realm
is in a dimension our essences experience
between lives and our souls resonate then?

What if angels really exist?
Or don't?

Angel Chorus

Angels we have heard on high
whine about our air supply.
Coughing in polluted air
declare, "Let's get the hell out of there!"

Encounters with Angels

Guardian Angel Get on Task....Please

Angels
hear me.
Give people wings–
flight.
Let their dreams soar,
be real.
Lighten
weight
of souls.
Free muses and
enlightenment,
reveal.

Heavy trip to Earth

Angels
do rain-wet wings
weigh you down, make flight hard?
Does weather leave you untouched or
just us?

Not From the Mouths of Angels

Angels
liberated,
don't startle virgins now.
Know earthly births require both
sexes.

Request

Hey
angel,
some stardust?
Or maybe just
hi?

I'm No Angel

Wings
for mind's
flight only–
body grounded, brain
down.

Wind Bells

Wind
whispers
echo bells;
tinkle angel
songs.

Angels wink bright stars
into dull, dark earthly eyes
so we shine within.

Projections Before Flight

You
fly the
red-eyed flight.
Red-eye mother
watches as you sleep,
prays for no turbulence
to wake you from your dreams.
Arms hold dreams close. Wings fly smoothly.
Sleep until landing and light of day.
Ground-safe, steady, walk with wings on firm earth.

Light Flashes

Lo!
star-glow
from angel
flashlights in the
night.

Angel Cinquain

Angels
bring to new heights
our hearts, our souls, our loves
for peace, joy, laughter, goodwill—well
most days.

Harbingers

Angels
wing-it
over my head,
watch
from surfaces,
survey
my life's
deeds.
Guard me,
protect me from harm,
guide my actions
and play.

Angels
bring light,
surround with joy,
life
spirits when times
darkle.
If I
wait,
listen,
pay attention,
poetry will
sparkle.

Angel Flights

Do angels hide in
cumulus crevices, peek
as airplanes fly by?

Can angels transform
thin as vapor, disappear
when humans wing it?

Why do angels flee
when earthbound beings soar,
struggling for flight.

Angels on the Internet

I can send angels by e-mail
no longer just by snail mail--
images of them winging,
sounds of magical singing,
profound messages bringing
solace, joy, peace, bell ringing.
Paper messages now just pale
unless the Internet should fail.

Angelic Tweeku

Angels
wing it by clueless
humans

Angels
still rock an emptied
cradle

Angels
must find some requests
boring

Angels
lift most wingless ones
to flight

Angels
see blood clots in
oil spills

Angels
shake complacency--
earthquakes

Angels
singe our conscience in
fire

Angels
empower hope with
feathers

Angels
use pennies as love
tokens

Modern Angels

Why do angels reside on a cloud?
Why do they sing off-key, out loud?
Why do they travel with wings
when technology brings
swifter flights, ear plugs
soft seats. plush rugs.
Adjust sites!
Smooth flights!
Right?

Playful angels roll
halos on bumpy. dark clouds,
dance hip-hop thunderously.

Angels in the Sand

They
flail
fan-like
arms and scrape
windshield-wipe legs to
make angels in sand before waves.

Modus Operandi

Angels' halos are hula hoops
her head–bright loops
swirly.

Angel's soft gossamer gown blows
over cloud flows
twirly.

Angel's song strummed with a harp
is never sharp–
lilting.

Angel's dance enhances her glow
but her halo's
tilting.

Angels Fly Away

Where angels fear to fly
their wings flit a fly-by.
Care given to clear the sky.
Share spirits when they try.

So why do they stay away?
Go when we fervently pray?
Sow goodness their own way?
Flow from our feet of clay?

They bring their own flight
day or just fly-by-night
weigh what they think is right
may leave us to our plight.

The Devil Laughed

Angels raced from white cloud to Earth.
They had a mission to bring mirth.
The challenge was folks didn't care.
The devil laughed at this affair.

The angels tried to wake folks up
to ditch the nay and hitch the yup.
They cloud-sat, chins in hand, midair.
The devil laughed at this affair.

The clouds all sank, heaving with rain
to dissipate with sun again,
but sun in Oregon is rare.
The devil laughed at this affair.

Angel Weavers

Angels weave the universe with light,
thread thoughts with golden glow.
We tangle in the knots, dull shine,
snag or tie what we know.

Angels are made of finer stuff-
so quarky, so unseen–
we rarely know they are around
or enter in our scene.

Angels shape-shift to our visions
of angelic presence,
then hang around just beyond our reach
dispensing their essence.

Angels have their own messages,
their own inward glory,
to needle, untangle light threads,
help us live our story.

Upswing

Angels, I'm weary, seeking some joy.
My spirit's limp, limbs achy.
Wing me along and sing me a song.
My thoughts are drifting, my grip shaky.

Angels, my comfort, my truth envoy
lift me up in thought and deed.
Sing me a song and wing me along.
Help me meet each being's urgent need.

Angels, what magic do you employ
to find ways to intervene?
Wing me along and sing me a song.
Support me to be a go-between.

Angels, what energies can you buoy
to give my essence a boost?
Sing me a song and wing me along.
Please see my lethargy gets vamoosed!

Dusting Off Angels

Angels are collecting lots of dust.
They're not on active duty.
Give me a dust rag–don't lollygag
it's time angels shared their beauty.

Angels are just hanging around now.
It's time for them to bring it.
Don't lollygag, give me a dust rag.
Angels have a message and sing it.

Angel voices are raspy–quite hoarse.
They've been off-duty too long.
Give me a dust rag. Don't lollygag.
Shake wings, angels and shout out your song.

Angel wings are now a-fluttering.
The whole bright room is a-buzz.
Don't lollygag. Put down the dust rag.
All's right now in heaven...just becuz.

Hosting Angels

Hang
swing,
warm, dry
from weather.
Create a climate
of love, hope, peace, joy, play and fun.
Create room to dream and to fly.
Texture and color
a place to
create
write
muse.

Join
me
to write
upon clouds
with clarity, light
to lift the spirits of mortals.
Explore dimensions, new worlds, realms,
realities–me under wing,
celestial friend.
We can soar.
I'll leave
all
here.

We
all
do leave
at our time.
I am so anxious
to see what I can't imagine,
to feel universe's pulses.
earthbound I'm heavy,
diminished,
leaden
damp,
dark

So
take
me, fly
me to light.
Wing me to my dreams.
Land my insights, thoughts.
share these words, enlighten, support
steward the light to all of us.
We need angels near.
Come closer.
Hear us.
Love
us.

Enlightening in a Room Full of Angels

Candles in the window welcome us and glow.
They tell us something that deep down we know
that with good friends creation will grow
now life will vibrate.

Angels on the walls, angels hang down on string.
lovely angels made of most anything.
Angel messengers joyfully bring
us blessings outright.

In angelic room like this we all can write.
Angels give us muses, some fresh insight.
These angels never squabble or fight
guided from above.

Light in whatever form helps us see and muse
and if we can't then we try to infuse
not to make sense but to amuse
dispersed with our love.

My
angels
they
visit
exquisite
while I
sleep.
Angels
presumed so
inanimate
animate,
display,
play,
whisper
gossip from
on high,
sing–
winging
it.

Rejoicing Amid My Angel Collection

I
stand
amid
some thousands.
These mini-angels
resonate molecules with me.

I
sing
and dance.
They're captive,
unmoved. Another
frequency, music of the spheres?

This
host
listens
in silence.
Static halos ring.
Wings want to clap but only watch.

I
wish
halos
rolled like hoops,
angels could be heard,
swing, fly and animate freely.

As
my
halo
tilts at a
rakish angle, what's
inanimate, invisible sustains.

Departures

Inconvenient Muse

My muse likes to wake me at three.
Turn on the light! Grab pen!
Reach for a notepad on the shelf quite near.
Jot the line hastily.
Writing's hard to read in morning–
not clear.

My muse likes to wake me at four.
Click the switch. Fumble pen.
Notepad drops. I tumble, stumble from bed.
I write a few lines more.
Groggily, I tried to record
what's said.

My muse likes to wake me at five.
Such a chatterbox muse!
Several times in each hour she'll come.
She pokes my brain alive
unraveling poetry lines–
welcome.

My muse likes to wake me at six.
Gets a tad annoying.
I am of agitated, foggy mind.
I need this muse-ful fix.
But I snooze fitfully, mindful
I find.

My muse wakes me up at seven
just before alarm.
I scratch down another line for her sake.
She invades dream heaven,
brings me back to Earth and poem
awake.

Launching a Poem

Will words land or take flight?
Land sounds to thud or sing?
Words sadden? Delight
readers? My poem ring?

Land sounds to thud or sing.
Line up words, bounce like notes–
musical rendering?
What beat the pace connotes?

Words sadden? Delight?
Hammer or quicken heart?
Connect? Give insight?
Unravel, fall apart?

Readers, my poems ring
uneven, blur views.
Word-play while pondering
life's dance, art or blues.

Subverse Verse

When struggling to write verse
you hope you won't make it worse
as you jot down words, write terse
lines that plod like a hearse.
Some thoughts you can't rehearse.
Try to remove the writer's block curse.
each form you need to nurse.
All fear you must disperse.
Mind and hand must converse.
Apathy you must reverse.
So many approaches, so diverse
it is easy to immerse,
so try not to be perverse.
Try to transverse
poems to the universe–
maybe reach the multiverse.

When You Write

Write a poem of light
so vision shines bright,
block dark words imprint,
let light words sprint,
win a mind raced
darkness chased
toward light.
Be free
to fly
wing
words
for
flight,
land
thoughts
to
touch grounded experience.

Winged Ones On My Mind

Birds
peck polluted
lawn. Clasp branches.

Butterflies
splay wings–
palettes of art.

Fairies
lasso slugs,
back at helm.

Angels
toss halos
to ring joy.

Believe
what's real,
what's otherworldly.

Books

Books
open,
flattened by hand,
stagnant as head
joins.

Books
are wings,
land in hands,
flap in mind and
fly.

Book Shelves

are
lips which
mouth words from
tooth-like bringing
smiles.

Poetry

Trying to nail Jello to a tree trunk is trying to define poetry.
(Robert Lewis)
What can be explained is not poetry. (Carl Sandburg)
When you talk to yourself it is poetry. (Hughes Mearns)
At its best a record of an inner song is written poetry. (Denise
Levertov)
A poem that begins in delight and ends in wisdom is poetry.
(Robert Frost)
The best words in the best order is poetry. (Samuel Taylor Coleridge)

Breathe-in experience, breathe-out poetry. (Muriel Rukeyser)
The music of the soul and about all great and feeling souls is
poetry. (Voltaire)
The moment of change is the only poem for poetry. (Adrienne Rich)
Prose of the intellect, the language of feeling is poetry. (Benedetto
Croce)
When the small hairs rise on the back of the neck it is poetry.
(William Rose Benet)
The clear expression of mixed feelings is poetry. (W.H. Auden)

The essence of invention is poetry.
Producing something unexpected, surprises, delights is poetry.
(Samuel Johnson)
So much a true work of the soul than prose is poetry.
Primarily a dialogue with the self is poetry. (May Sarton)
Being literalists of the imagination is poetry. (Marianne Moore)
When they extend the language it is poetry. (Kurt Vonnegut)

Not the rose, but the scent of the rose is poetry.
Not the sky, but the light of the sky is poetry.
Not the fly, but the gleam of the fly is poetry.
Not the sea, but the sound of the sea is poetry.
Not myself, but what makes me is poetry.
Who knows what is poetry? (Eleanor Farjeon)

The theorem of a yellow silk handkerchief is poetry
when knotted with riddles is poetry
sealed in a balloon tied to a kite is poetry
flying in a white wind against a blue sky is poetry. (Carl Sandburg)
Searching for syllables to shoot at barriers is poetry --
barriers of the unknown and the unknowable is poetry. (Carl Sandburg)

When a poem makes your toenails twinkle it's poetry. (e.e. cummings)
Be more authentic, lessen anxiety, tell the truth with poetry. (Rita Dove)
Become more tender to each other with poetry. (Maya Angelou)
The crunch of jostling ice floes, two nightingales dueling is poetry. (Boris Pasternak)
Nothing less than the perfect speech and to utter truth is poetry. (Matthew Arnold)
A spine trying to go on without any background into chaos and cliche is poetry.
(William Carlos Williams)

Ancient Greeks in the Olympics combined sport and poetry.
Perfection of the body and intellect required poetry.
Around the world in all cultures through the ages there's been poetry.
In all facets of modern life there is poetry.
In music, slams, readings, books, on-line, with media there is poetry.
In myriad of forms poets can create dynamic new poetry.

Seek the poetry Muses. Poetry delights and infuses light.
Poetry expresses one's soul. Poetry plays an important role
for poetry seeks to create and educate so all can appreciate poetry.

I have dined with kings, I've been offered wings and I've never been too impressed. Bob Dylan

Intelligence without ambition is a bird without wings. Salvador Dali

Fly without wings, dream without open eyes. Dejan Stojanovic

Time is swift. it races by. Opportunities are born and die...still you wait and will not try. A bird who dares not rise and fly. A.A. Milne

There are only two lasting bequests we can give our children—one is roots, the other wings. Stephen Covey

If you were born without wings, do nothing to prevent them from growing. Coco Chanel

Acknowledgments:

Published Poems Appeared in:

Red Cape Capers (Chapbook)
Cinqueries
Fibs and Other Truths
Black Stars on a White Sky
Poems That Count
Poems That Count Too
Syllables of Velvet (www.rainbowcommunications.org)
Word-Playful (www.rainbowcommunications.org)

About Linda Varsell Smith:
You never know what's going to happen. We're not going to rehearse—we're just going to wing it. Garrison Starr

Since childhood I have had a fascination with wings. From the earliest tales of fairies told by my father, I have imagined winged creatures and winged thought.

Since childhood I have written poems and stories. I created comic books of creatures on other planets, created fantasies with dolls and paper dolls.

I have collected owls, perhaps hoping for wisdom. I have collected fairies and most recently focused on my collection of angels in many media.

Wings on solid or ephemeral beings, wings of thought and musings,

I am surrounded by wings and enjoy winging it.

Ideas have wings. No one can stop their flight. Unknown

Linda Varsell Smith teaches Creative Writing and Children's Literature at Linn-Benton Community College, edits for Calyx Books since 1982, former President of the Oregon Poetry Association and current President of PEN Women—Portland Branch. She's published seven poetry books and twelve fantasy novels.

www.ingramcontent.com/pod-product-compliance
Lightning Source LLC
LaVergne TN
LVHW091252080426
835510LV00007B/224